THE HEALER'S BURDEN

The Healer's Burden: Stories and Poems of Professional Grief brings to the fore the feelings of end-of-life professionals as they daily face dying and death. Such workers will find their grief—heretofore disenfranchised—now validated. While this alone is so valuable, they can also find strategies to cope with the inevitable experience, yet often hidden, of the impact of loss and grief. Given the current pandemic, this book could not have arrived at a more needed time. It is a mandated read for seasoned and beginning health carers now working in that thin space between life and death.

KENNETH J. DOKA, PHD
Senior Consultant, The Hospice Foundation of America
Author, *Disenfranchised Grief, Grief Is a Journey*

Modern medicine has never yearned more than for a book like this. *The Healer's Burden* allows us to get in touch with our passion for healing and recognizes the pain that often walks beside it. Finding the true meaning and purpose in our daily work is critical to our overall well-being, mitigates burnout and promotes our sustainability in medicine. These personal stories and poems create a relatable narrative. As we work to be in the here and now, taking a moment to read an excerpt, reflect upon it and create our own narrative can not only heal us but also connect us with both our patients and our colleagues and remind us why we entered medicine in the first place.

LISA MACLEAN, MD
Associate Professor
Director of Physician Wellness
Henry Ford Health System

My very first nursing job was in the intensive care unit at a large academic health science hospital. Since I was new, it was my job to work the Christmas and New Year holidays. On Christmas day, we had eleven patients. By New Year's Day, all eleven had died. I was distraught and did not know how to deal with my emotions. I asked myself if this was the right position for me. Could I really handle all this death? I could not remember any lecture in nursing school that prepared me for death and my emotions.

Although I came to learn that being with people at the time of their death is a unique privilege given only to a few, the hidden burden that health care professionals feel takes its toll on body, mind, and spirit. Much has been written about the moral distress and the compassion fatigue experienced by those who care for the dying. *The Healer's Burden: Stories and Poems of Professional Grief*, offers much needed compelling insights through personal reflections of professionals from various disciplines who work with the dying. Through stories and poems, the book provides an unparalleled resource to professionals to deal with their own personal grief journey. The book is a must read for all in the field of caring for the dying.

PATRICIA GONCE MORTON, PHD, RN, ACNP-BC, FAAN
Dean Emeritus, University of Utah College of Nursing
Editor, *Journal of Professional Nursing*

Professional caregivers experience grief at the loss of those in their care. These stories and poems by chaplains, doctors, nurses, respiratory therapists, social workers, and a therapeutic clown attest to the weightiness of watching patients suffer and die and wishing they could have "done more." In crafting these deeply felt experiences into well told stories, and placing them on the page, they honor the singular lives of people they cared for. Readers come to know both the givers and receivers of care and, often, to recognize themselves in these encounters with life and death.

Editors have wisely and generously included guidelines for using narrative methods to engage with these stories, affording readers opportunities to reclaim their right as healers to heal themselves.

LYNNE MIJANGOS, RN, LMSW, MFA, MS
Lecturer in Narrative Medicine
Columbia University
Co-editor, *Narrative Social Work: The Power and Possibility of Story*

I completed my specialty training with a tremendous sense of pride, prepared to have a great impact on patients and families in their time of greatest need and hopelessness. I entered and ended each day with the knowledge that I had given my all, but, like many of my colleagues, I ignored fatigue and underestimated the accumulated trauma of those occasions when, despite my best efforts, the neurological disease won. *The Healer's Burden* is a book of intimate stories and poems from healthcare providers experiencing professional grief. It serves as a powerful tool to help us listen, learn, and heal so that we have the courage to continue helping others in need. We must remember we are never alone. And we must find hope even in the darkest moments, for the lessons learned can give us insights into how to bring light to others.

TONY AVELLINO, MD, MBA
Pediatric Neurosurgeon
MSU Health Care Chief Clinical and Medical Officer
Michigan State University

Professional grief often expresses itself as "I am tired…" But grief should not be confused with exhaustion, and these stories and poems should not be confused with simple tales. *The Healer's Burden* is a collection of self-reflections that completes the professional grief mantra of "I am tired," with "yet I have a community with whom I can share the weight." Every clinician who reads this book will feel their burden lighten, since these stories and poems give their readers the sense that others are helping to carry the load.

IRA BEDZOW, PHD
Director of the Biomedical Ethics and Humanities Program
UNESCO Chair in Bioethics
New York Medical College

This rich collection of voices demonstrates the tremendous power of personal accounts of human experiences. Each author creates a window. For some readers, this window will be into their own souls. This book will help them to name and understand their own experiences with professional grief. For others, this collection will enable them to better appreciate the burden of loss professionals face. *The Healer's Burden* shines much-needed light into the hidden space of professional grief.

ANA S. ILTIS, PHD
Carlson Professor of University Studies and Professor of Philosophy
Director, Center for Bioethics, Health and Society
Co-editor, *Narrative Inquiry in Bioethics*

THE HEALER'S BURDEN

The Healer's Burden: Stories and Poems of Professional Grief is published by
The University of Iowa Carver College of Medicine in Iowa City, Iowa.

THE HEALER'S BURDEN

STORIES AND POEMS OF PROFESSIONAL GRIEF

MELISSA FOURNIER AND GINA PRIBAZ, EDITORS

Roy J. and Lucille A. Carver College of Medicine
University of Iowa, Iowa City, IA

CONTENTS

FOREWORD Rana Awdish   i

PREFACE Melissa Fournier   v

       Gina Pribaz   viii

SECTION ONE

  ADMISSION Jennifer Hu   3

  SILENT INTERCESSION Hui-wen Alina Sato   5

  HELPING YOU Simone Kantola   9

  NIGHT SHIFT Aneesh Rajmaira   15

  UNMASKING GRIEF Maria Wolfe   17

  THE FORMULA FOR WHOLENESS Katherine DiBella Seluja   25

  AND NOW I KNOW I WILL NEVER Katherine DiBella Seluja   27

  TOUGH HAND Richard Morand   29

  ELEGY IN AN O.R. LOCKER ROOM Daniel J. Waters   35

  SECTION 1 DISCUSSION AND PROMPTS   37

SECTION TWO

  LIKE ANY GOOD TRICK Daniel Becker   43

  SPIDER-MAN Anna-leila Williams   45

  A RAPID DECLINE Thom Schwarz   47

  MEDICINE: A HAUNTING Christopher Blake   51

  HAIR CLIPS FOR ESMA Lila Flavin   55

  TRAUMA BAY Shannon Arntfield   63

  GRAVITY Paivi E. Pittman   65

  SHELF LIFE Howard F. Stein   67

  SURROUNDED Pamela A. Mitchell   69

  SECTION 2 DISCUSSION AND PROMPTS   71

SECTION THREE

FALL, THEN WINTER Kacper Niburski   77

CADUCEUS, TREE OF KNOWLEDGE Sheri Reda   79

THE ANGIO Serena J. Fox   81

FROM BOTH SIDES NOW Elena Schwolsky   83

AMAZING GRACE Rondalyn Varney Whitney   89

FINDING WHAT'S LOST Mary C. Lindberg   91

OCCUPATIONAL THERAPY Veneta Masson   95

THE GOLD STARS Lara Ronan   97

COPY/KÄTHE KOLLWITZ Kelley White   101

SECTION 3 DISCUSSION AND PROMPTS   103

SECTION FOUR

A TRIBUTE (AND HOMAGE TO E E CUMMINGS) Pam Lenkov   109

NAMELESS Rachel Fleishman   111

PASSING THROUGH Joseph Bocchicchio   115

YOU LEAVE THE ROOM William A. French   125

A BIT IN THE TEETH Jafar Al-Mondhiry   127

A BEAUTIFUL MESS Teegan Mannion   133

FOR AIR Jennifer Hu   141

SECTION 4 DISCUSSION AND PROMPTS   143

CONTRIBUTOR BIOGRAPHIES   146

A GUIDE FOR USING *THE HEALER'S BURDEN* IN GROUPS   153

WORKS CITED   155

ACKNOWLEDGMENTS   156

ABOUT THE EDITORS   157

ABOUT THE ARTIST   158

FOREWORD

There was a time during my critical care fellowship, after nearly bleeding to death from an occult liver tumor, that I lost language. I had lost other things during that long and fraught ICU admission. I had lost a baby, my dignity, functional kidneys, and any semblance of independence, but it was the loss of language that was most disruptive to my identity. Without words, I was not sure I knew who or what I was. Losing the ability to communicate was isolating in a disorienting way that left me outside of my own life.

To regain myself, I knew I would have to recover my lost words. And to lure them back, I had to approach them gently. If I chased too hard, they scattered like children in a game of tag. I have found many things in life are like this; if you look directly at something, you cannot draw the knowing toward you. It is often best to triangulate on a third thing. My grief was like that. A thing I had to approach from other angles—poetry, books, and paintings—before I could understand it in any coherent way.

The process of sitting in quiet reflection with other people's words, and eventually beginning to write about my experiences, allowed me, over time, to find cohesion and even wholeness. Writing became an act of rebuilding, and of sense-making. What I could not have known was that spending time in that difficult, broken place, following the recursive line of healing back into myself until I could re-emerge, would train me to see differently. I could now see the things I had been unable to look at honestly—the dysfunction ingrained in the culture of medicine and the way that it so often failed the most vulnerable. The way it had failed me, even as it saved my life. That both things could be true. It had saved me, and it had broken me. I had very likely been perpetuating the same harm.

I fell backward into the therapeutic space of narrative medicine. The pain of losing language led me to other people's words. Other people's words provided a safe space for me to heal. Healing brought my words back to me. My words became a book, and my book became a third thing for others, which enabled them to heal. Everything is reciprocal. Or, as my mom says, "The world is very round."

Which brings me back to medicine and to *The Healer's Burden*, this book that casts light on one of healthcare's last hidden liabilities: professional grief. The inadequacies in the system not only damage our patients but hurt the healers as well. Medicine lacks built-in spaces to do the work of grieving, though grief is at times the only constant. The grief of our patients, the grief of their families, the grief of our colleagues, and our own splintering grief. Perhaps it is the pervasive nature of grief that makes it invisible to us, makes it the thing that is easiest to not see. It is our air, and we mistakenly believe that the air will not drown us. That belief, that unique hubris, is so often our undoing. Unattended grief is the unspoken and unacknowledged cause of death for so many that medicine has lost. Knowing this means we must take responsibility for changing it.

For years, I have kept the poem "Things Shouldn't Be So Hard" by Kay Ryan above my desk, to remind me to soften in the hard places. To remind me to mourn even the quiet and expected losses. Ryan writes, "The passage / of a life should show; / it should abrade." (40) The lives we tend and lose leave abrasions; things shouldn't be so hard, but they are. In connection to Ryan's and others' words, to others' narratives, we can soften. We can tend our own abrasions. But we need help in doing so. Developing narrative competence, the ability to listen in order to interpret and act on the stories of others (Charon, *JAMA* 1897), is perhaps the most essential skill we need our health care providers to possess, if we wish for empathic, whole humans. If we dare to wish for joy in work.

This is why *The Healer's Burden* is such a joy to behold. What my illness made available to me, and what I hear echoed in these pages, is an awareness of the true healing potential of our shared humanity and the innate value of our presence in the lives of others. In my book *In Shock*, I wrote that we often imagine we have the power to stand at the chasm of death, our backs to its void, and heroically catch our patients as they hurl themselves toward it. But with faith in the meaning of our presence we can and should turn with our patients to face the chasm together. We should turn with them and acknowledge its vastness and darkness. This book offers yet another turning that requires faith in the meaning of presence. A turning toward one another as a community of grievers who have borne witness to the inevitability of the chasm. By their willingness to be vulnerable, the writers featured in this collection, who represent a broad range of disciplines and experiences, have begun to create this community. And by crafting thoughtful discussion questions and writing prompts, the editors intentionally issue an invitation for readers to join in the turning.

Reckoning with grief is no small task. But ignoring it is no longer necessary.

RANA AWDISH, MD
Author, *In Shock: My Journey From Death to Recovery and the Redemptive Power of Hope*

PREFACE

She walked into the house most evenings at seven-thirty calling out a hopeful greeting followed by a deep sigh. I knew better than to ask her for anything in those moments, but my younger sister never quite caught on. "Mom, I need you to drive me to the store to get a poster board for my project that's due tomorrow." My mother was a cardiac intensive care nurse who often worked twelve-hour shifts days in a row. The last thing she wanted to deal with was the hassle of dinner and poster boards and the multiple needs of five children. Of course, this was long before a text message could prompt a quick-fix stop on the way home. This was back when nurses wore caps, starched white uniforms, white hose, and pristinely polished shoes.

As a matter of conversation, my mom would sometimes share stories of her patients' distress or the number of deaths in a given week, but mostly to either make a point about the dangers of smoking and alcohol or to highlight her exhaustion. One night, minutes after she'd settled into bed, the phone rang and I answered. "Mom, it's the hospital." My mother, alarmed and ashamed, raced back to the unit, a forty-five minute drive from our house into the heart of Detroit, to return the narcotics key she'd inadvertently left in her pocket. She was mortified by her error; she was the type of employee who was always punctual, always responsible, and never called in sick. When I was thirteen and my father died, she went to work the following morning without telling us of his death, leaving my stepfather the task of bearing bad news. This did not strike me as odd until my own daughter was thirteen and I flashed back to myself at that age. As a mother, I could not imagine anything more important than being there for my child in the face of such tragedy.

Years passed before I understood the challenges my mother faced, the demands of her work, and its impact on her life and ours. When, at forty, I began working as a hospice social worker, my experiences of caring for patients at the end of life lent a clarity to my vision of my mother not unlike that which occurs after wind dies down, turbulent waters calm, and one can see clearly to the lake bed. I began to understand the heaviness that constant exposure to death places on the heart, mind, and soul; how even supportive work environments struggle to adequately meet the needs of employees engaged in emotional labor when operating as corporate entities following tight business models; and how challenging it is to remember that a child's poster board is as important to her in the moment as a dose of morphine or calling in the family is to a dying patient. I became aware of the weight of the burdens my mother carried as my own grew heavier.

While I was well aware of burnout, compassion fatigue, secondary trauma, and the importance of combating these, it wasn't until working as the program director for a bereavement center when I came across an article by Dr. Elizabeth J. Clark, a leader in the field of social work and palliative care, that I encountered the term *professional grief.* "Professional grief usually takes the form of hidden grief—grief that is internalized and not openly expressed," Dr. Clark wrote. "There is no natural outlet for it, and the demands of work overshadow it. This lack of expression may result in cumulative grief, or what sometimes is referred to as bereavement overload. This can further lead to a legacy of vulnerability, burnout, or post-traumatic stress reaction." (Clark 936) I thought of my mother and her inability to be present with me when my father died. I thought of my internal and outward reactions to the deaths of the patients I'd accompanied—infants, teens, and adults—and how so many of them remained present with me in unique and difficult ways. I thought of the responsibility we have to one another as we work in high-loss environments to pause and make space for our own grief, and I knew in that moment, as a social worker and a writer, I would commit myself to doing so.

At the time we editors released our call for submissions for this book, COVID-19 had not yet shown itself. In fact, submissions were due well before any lockdowns in the United States. Since that time, stories and images of the impact of the pandemic on healthcare workers have emerged, raising public awareness of the effects of so much death and despair. But it shouldn't take a pandemic to highlight the need for healthcare systems to tend the bereavement needs of professionals exposed to continuous loss. Nor should that tending end if and when the COVID-19 crisis resolves. The needs of aides, clergy, nurses, first responders, doctors, social workers, medical students, and trainees will continue as long as patients die, of whatever causes, and the conversation around how best to address those needs is only just beginning.

I am often asked, as I know others in the field are, *How do you do this work?* Sometimes my response is glib: *It's the only thing I know how to do and I'm really bad with numbers.* Other times, I share the story of walking a Florida shoreline with my brother.

While in my thirties, my oldest brother and I found ourselves on the beach during a time in his life when he was in the midst of personal transformation. It was a special encounter for us, and I knew I'd want to remember it. As we walked and talked, I collected as mementos stones I found along the way—first, I held a few in one hand, then a few in both, and then I made a hammock of my shirt in which I carried several. Before long, the stones began spilling out as I walked. I bent down to retrieve them until my efforts became futile and I simply couldn't carry any more. At that point, I set them all down and stopped collecting, leaving them on the shoreline where they belonged. As we continued walking, I would pick one up, turn it over in my hands to study it, comment on its features, and place it down again.

For me, each death encountered in the work environment is not unlike a beach stone. We can pick it up, examine it, appreciate its singularity, and place it down before walking on, but it is futile to try and carry them all. My hope is that in reading and discussing the stories and poems in this book, and that in writing in the shadow of what is presented here, we can hold our stones up to the light and then gently set them down.

MELISSA FOURNIER
For my mother, Mary Ann Rohde, RN
and Elizabeth J. Clark, PhD, ACSW, MPH, who died May 23, 2020

Maybe this is a heavy book. Even its birth, in a manner of speaking, is tied to death.

To illustrate how this book might help lift the weight it witnesses, come back with me five years to the airy lobby of the neuroscience building at the University of Iowa, where I'm attending The Examined Life medical humanities conference. I'm balancing a plate of tacos in one hand, my bags and bundles in the other. In my head a phrase is echoing, one that you might have heard if you've ever encountered the narrative medicine work of Dr. Rita Charon, whose keynote in the adjacent auditorium moments ago offered the idea of storytelling as "creating a clearing" (Charon, Introduction 5) where people can come together as equals and share something of themselves. I spy an open spot at an anonymous round table and introduce myself to strangers who will soon become friends (a few years down the line, one of them will invite me to coedit this anthology with her) largely because of a conversation we open and enter into together.

It could have been about any topic that plunges us into murky water where we can't touch bottom, but this particular conversation is about end-of-life ethics. We talk about death, which means we also discuss a good deal about life, what is most important to us, and how we weigh and measure these things. In terms of the backgrounds, beliefs, and politics of the speakers, we are all over the place. And we don't hold back. We have no obligation to delve, no bonds to one another, no particular reason to risk embarrassment or aggravation, and yet here we are, with a providential grace, "going there." When the tacos are crumbs and it is time to find our next break-out sessions, we slowly push in our chairs and marvel aloud at what has just happened.

What did happen? First, a disclaimer. I just described, rather broadly, a conversation, which is only a cousin of storytelling. But when well done, both rely on a thoughtful curation of words, and both hinge on a certain disposition characterized by the courage to be real—eloquence rooted in honesty. What happened at that table, and what I am driving at in the preface of an anthology about professional grief, is what can happen when we allow ourselves to trust others with our deeply felt and difficult experiences by shaping them into words only we can say. Then we honor that same impulse in the person who takes a seat beside us, and together we engage in the generosity of story.

As Arthur Frank explains in *The Wounded Storyteller*, "The moral genius of storytelling is that each, teller and listener, enters the space of the story for the other." (Frank 18) The writers and poets who have contributed to this book have bravely entered the space of professional grief. They help "create a clearing" for a subject long closed off in healthcare, one that many would rather try to drape or downplay. So we start this anthology with "Admission," a prose poem from Jennifer Hu that offers an iconic image of this ultimately inadequate tendency to try to veil death and its attendant grief: "—and every which way I pulled it, the curtain never hid enough," she writes.

Hui-wen Alina Sato's "Silent Intercession" and Maria Wolfe's "Unmasking Grief" pull the curtain back further on the futility of denying grief even as they search for ways to process and witness it. In "Tough Hand," Richard Morand brings readers into a trauma bay just after a code: "Now the room is silent as if nothing at all occurred. I stand watching the red stain forming on the pristine white sheet, mocking me in my failure." His essay voices the painful complexity of a surgeon's bold move toward an honest grappling with the limits of his profession and his practice.

Being "haunted" by loss is a theme that develops strongly in the second section of the book. Christopher Blake's imaginative "Medicine: A Haunting" uses the form of a ghost story to externalize a nagging inner voice that whispers recriminations in the ear of a young doctor seeking solitude on an island. We see his mental struggle to understand his experience: "The human mind fears entropy. It seeks order. It seeks patterns where there are none because patterns mean information, the difference between life and death." The mind plays tricks. Poet Shannon Arntfield's "Trauma Bay" shows a trainee's vulnerability in a fearful identification with a devastated car-wreck victim as she makes her secondary examination: "My tears come and I / have to look away. Your face / is not your face."

Strategies and rituals to cope with professional grief, especially when that grief reopens personal wounds, feature in section three. Here an eighteen-hour surgery to save a thirteen-year-old trips Kacper Niburski into a childhood memory in which his teacher asks him to write about the loss of a classmate. Many years later, he is still writing it. Serena J. Fox's poem "The Angio" uses the image of the white coat as a carry-all for family and patient experiences that jumble together. Speaking of her father, the speaker says: "I did not want to/bring him here, because I did not want him to/know how easily he fits into my pocket..." Elena Schwolsky's poignant "From Both Sides Now" chronicles the experiences of a nurse persevering in a pediatric AIDS unit while her own husband is dying from the disease.

In the fourth section we read about patients and caregivers on the edge of seemingly insurmountable hopelessness. In his poem "You Leave the Room," William French hints at the desire to walk away when you "feel only the urgent thrust / of your own blood / as it surges along the endless / circuit, sustaining life by looping / through an uncaring heart." The strain of being a therapeutic clown on a children's oncology ward in "A Beautiful Mess" has Teegan Mannion's narrator thinking about stepping back from her work to care for her own bruised heart.

Joseph Bocchicchio's "Passing Through" and Rachel Fleishman's "Nameless" render systemic social injustice personal and show how it contributes to the sense of despair that assails those tasked to care for vulnerable patients. What does it mean "to care" at all?

Questions like this that arise from these poems and stories have no simple answers, but it is better to ask them than to let them go unspoken and smoldering. To help facilitate inquiry and conversation, we have arranged the book into these four thematic sections, each capped by a series of discussion questions and writing prompts. These have been carefully designed for individual self-reflection or for use by groups of healthcare professionals and educators to work through with colleagues or students, perhaps somewhere at a round table together. A facilitation guide is provided at the back of this book.

In his wonderful 1988 essay, "The Singular First Person," Scott Russell Sanders explains why he feels called to offer his voice to readers: "I choose to write about my experience not because it is mine, but because it seems to me a door through which others might pass." (Sanders 667) It is our hope that the stories and poems in *The Healer's Burden*, along with the discussions and writings this book generates, will help those who work on the frontlines open a door to a space in which it is safe to explore the grief that naturally accumulates while working in high-loss environments. If we expect healthcare professionals to be fully present and see their patients as whole human beings, we must afford them the same care.

GINA PRIBAZ

SECTION ONE

ADMISSION

JENNIFER HU

—and every which way I pulled it, the curtain never hid enough. And every time we spoke, our voices traveled over the curtain so the others could hear your private fears. I was ill equipped against my feeble and false hope. You already knew you were dying. Your body was announcing it.

I was walking around the curtain. I was holding it aside for the nurse. I was circling it around the IV lines. We listened to its metal rattle. "I'm sorry," I said, referring to the curtain's inadequacy. "I'm sorry," I said, referring to all that you had not been told yet.

Then they brought you upstairs, your bed pushed behind another curtain, the door slightly ajar, the light pale. And every time I walked by your room, I saw your face, your deep black eyes, the curtain trying to hide you, still inadequately, the curtain fluttering, from our breaths, the overhead vent, the other bodies that still could move and were not yours and crossed, too easily, the space between—

SILENT INTERCESSION

HUI-WEN ALINA SATO

It was my turn to pray. I felt fine. I really did. Work and home life had been relatively steady as of late, and I wasn't feeling particularly tender about anything. I was with a small group of mothers who gathered in the same living room twice a month to pray for our children, their friends, families, teachers, and administrators at our local elementary school. It was my turn to pray when she came to mind as she sometimes had in recent months. Sometimes the image was that of her in the photo taped just above the head of her hospital bed, the one with her cheek to cheek with her mother, both their broad smiles lit up for the camera, both their eyes sparkling with mischief. This time, however, the image in my mind was that of her lying all too still in her hospital bed, eyes closed, face swollen to an unnatural size, the purple bruised hue in her skin undeniable even in the dimly lit room. She would have been in fourth grade this year on campus with our kids, had it not been for the accident that claimed her life over the summer. She breathed her last breaths in our unit.

It was my turn to pray, and really I felt fine.

Sure, my personal boundaries had been stretched when I realized after her death that this girl had been a student at my daughter's school. I'd been browsing our school's social media page when I suddenly clapped my hand to my mouth. There, in the midst of enthusiastic updates about the start of the school year, was that same photo of her and her mother in a somber note announcing her death. All that time she was a patient in our unit, I had no idea how many connections I shared with her and her family. Still I felt fine, and just thought it important to pray for the girl's loved ones as they navigated the new reality of life without her. But in simply uttering her name, I unlocked the door to the hidden place where I sequester grief when it refuses to behave. I felt my body heave with the force of grief emerging, asserting its presence. Startled, my mind went blank except for the clear thought that this sudden flood of grief was about the girl who should have been in fourth grade, but it wasn't just about her.

It was about the extraordinarily terrible summer our unit had had. About the family in town on vacation who would find themselves bewildered, flying home lost without their child after a sudden illness erased her name from the returning passenger list. Our summer with multiple deaths from car accidents and suicide attempts and child abuse that ended up on the evening news. Our summer with patients who felt relatively safe on their cancer floors but less safe in our ICU because they had heard this is where the cancer kids go at the end. It was about the startling reality that these patients perceive me as the nurse who comes to them when they are about to die. It was about my fear, always sitting just below the surface, that I could one day be the mother at the bedside and not the nurse.

It was about my feeling strangely unfamiliar in this posture of prayer that had once felt so familiar, feeling disoriented about who God was and who I was as someone who initially wanted to do His work through nursing. I thought I knew what I was signing up for. Naïve as it may seem, I wanted to be a vessel of God's healing, comfort, and hope when I became a nurse. But the vagueness of these terms became apparent when I could not heal the damage the traumas inflicted, when my efforts at comfort felt fleeting at best and insultingly futile at worst, when I struggled to put substance into offered hope that didn't feel like anything more than platitudes.

It was about my faith being put through the fire, rendered speechless by the pain I felt in its refining. I watched so many visitors come to my patients' bedsides with a discomfiting level of joy and confidence as they prayed over my neurologically devastated patients. We believe in You, God, to do miracles! Bring healing and raise up this child from this bed! My faith felt so small and sad in comparison with that of these unshakable visitors. Yet at the same time I knew my hesitations about their intercession weren't blasphemous. This tension had been building in me as a Christian nurse for some time, laced with hints of shame. I didn't know where to begin reconciling it until a wise pastor gently asked me, "Is this a question of different magnitudes of faith, or is it actually just a question of different expectations?"

My tearful silence was about my deep struggle to articulate what expectations should emerge, then, out of a faith that was being profoundly challenged and reshaped, and what prayers should flow out of those expectations. What am I to expect and ask of God when I look to Him to help these patients, to help us who survive what they do not survive as we tremble from the aftershocks of their deaths?

I heard my friends listening for me to go on with my prayer. I heard myself stifle my sobs.

I felt the tender gaze of God on me. I felt I'd known Him for a long time now. I could tell so many stories of all the things He has seen me through, all the reasons I'd come to love and trust Him. But it was my turn to pray for this girl's friends and family, for all of our children, and I simply dropped my eyes from Him and sobbed.

I want to pray for our children, but I'm not quite sure what to ask of You.
I am still finding my words.

HELPING YOU
SIMONE KANTOLA

When I first meet you in clinic, I catch myself staring at your teeth. I am perched on my rolling stool directly opposite you, and you are slouching in the corner chair, mouth hanging partly open. Each time I make eye contact with you, your teeth are in my field of vision. Nubby and uneven, they have the color and variegation of russet potatoes.

Your teeth instantly raise a number of questions. Do you ever brush them? Are they painful? How long since you last saw a dentist? And, primarily, what was the colorectal surgeon thinking, the one who sent you to me? In my estimation, a person's teeth reflect the general condition of their tissues as well as their self-care habits. Your teeth practically scream POOR OPERATIVE CANDIDATE.

But, it's not just your teeth. There's an abundance of reasons why no one wants to operate on you, why you've been passed over by surgeons for the past couple years. You're in your late forties, but you look so much older; neglect from your intellectual disability and mental illness has taken its toll. You live alone, and you have no friends; you don't even want to bother your only brother. You survive on just a monthly disability check. The clothes you wear are old and stained. I can't find anything going in your favor.

I am a reconstructive surgeon, and one of the colorectal surgeons here at the hospital has sent you to see me because you have a giant abdominal hernia. Over the past couple years, it has grown larger and larger, to the point where it now completely displaces your abdominal muscles. I read this in your medical chart, and still, it's even bigger than it sounds. When I lift your sweatshirt, I see your abdominal wall replaced by a bulging pile of bowels, writhing like snakes under a thin covering of stretched skin. It's the biggest hernia I've ever seen outside of a textbook.

I wrestle with conflicting thoughts. You have a bona fide problem. At one point, as an enthusiastic medical student, I chose to be a surgeon for opportunities like this to permanently fix people's problems. But I am tired now, and one person can only take on so many problems. Everything about your case will require substantially more work for me and my team, and what will it all be for if your hernia quickly recurs from your poor tissue quality or lack of self-care?

I decide to try to dissuade you from surgery by giving you an exceedingly long and thorough explanation of all the risks. I wax poetic about the potential wound breakdown, fluid collections, bleeding, infection, high chance of recurrence, side effects of anesthesia…even death.

You listen, face unmoving, then simply say, "Can you help me, doc?"

I have fallen silent. I feel, stirring inside, the sensitive part of me, the one which surgery has systematically tried to stifle. *He's had such a hard life. Look at the huge, painful problem he has. And yet, somehow, he has this childlike faith.* My heart begins to hurt for you.

Yes, I can probably help you, and helping you is probably going to cost me. But, this seems true as well, and it's what I latch on to: If I don't help you, no one will.

"Can you quit smoking?" I hear myself say.

"Yeah," you say. It comes out short, like a grunt.

"Okay," I say, and I shake your hand.

·   ·   ·

To be honest, I don't actually expect you to do it. I know that people with mental illness have higher rates of smoking and nicotine addiction for a reason—it helps with their symptoms. But, over the next six months, despite my expecting you to fail, you complete all the assignments I give you: quitting smoking, walking for exercise, drinking protein shakes, getting preoperative clearance.

As you complete each assignment, my nurses and I start to cheer you on. We start looking forward to your visits. We start making extra phone calls to make sure you remember you're coming to see us and check that your rides are set up. We start saving our meal vouchers and giving them to you, so you can stock up on food at the cafeteria.

Pulmonary function testing is your last step. I insist on it because I'm concerned that stuffing all your bowels back into your abdomen will push up too much on your lungs and compromise their function. I know your lungs have already been damaged by years of smoking, but I'd like to know the extent. A good report will be a green light; a bad report, the last possible offramp before surgery.

You aren't able to understand the instructions. You can't figure out how to keep a good seal on the mouthpiece or when to inhale or exhale at full force. You get frustrated with all the do-overs. The report comes back inconclusive.

I consider the offramp. Six months ago, I would have taken it, but I don't want to take it anymore. I know a repeat test won't yield any more information, so I just have to make a final decision.

You've done everything I've asked of you, against the odds. I choose to do everything I can for you.

.   .   .

Your surgery, the piecing back together and reinforcing of your abdominal wall, is difficult and takes my partner and I nearly eight hours to complete. There are moments when we doubt that we can get the hernia closed, and I worry that we might be making things worse. Numerous times, because of how hard we are pushing and pulling, I worry about your lungs. As we cinch in place the huge piece of mesh that corrals your bowels, I worry about how much pain you'll be in afterwards. When we finish the case and I finally take off my surgical gown, my scrubs are entirely soaked in sweat.

I'm still tired from the effort the next morning when I visit you in the Intensive Care Unit. It's Saturday and a little past 8:30 a.m.

"Hi," I say, coming into your room. "How was your night?" I close the privacy curtain behind me.

All around your bed are EKG leads and IV lines, threatening to entangle you. Your body remains still, but you turn your head. Since your facial expression is flat, I can't tell at a glance whether you're in pain.

"How are you feeling?" I say.

"Good," you grunt.

"Any pain?"

"No."

I wait for more, but you just stare back. The silence has become normal now.

I glance at the computer monitor above your bed. Your heartbeat is steady, your blood pressure is normal, and your oxygenation is on target. I am relieved.

"I've got good news," I say. I wonder whether you'll be able to guess. The high-pitched beeps of the oxygen sensor count out the seconds before you respond.

"Did it work?" you ask, and your eyes open wider.

I nearly whoop. I can't contain my smile. Reaching for the edge of your hospital gown, I reveal to you the new smoothness of your belly.

When I do, a little upward tug at the corners of your lips reveals the tips of your stained teeth. You are smiling. You're smiling! It's the first smile I've ever seen on you.

.   .   .

After visiting you, I am still smiling as I walk the four blocks from the hospital to home. It is drizzling outside, but I don't care. I am feeling thankful that, despite all the effort it took, your case was a success. I am still savoring your smile when my pager buzzes against my hip. The message is from my resident: "[You] coding. ICU doing chest compressions."

I run back over the wet pavement, through the double glass doors, and up the stairs. I am panting when I arrive to find your room packed with providers, all trying to get you back. Your lips and face are already grey as the Northwest sky.

I lean against the ICU's far window ledge, hidden behind a line of folded wheelchairs. Ten feet away, nurses are flitting in and out of other patients' rooms; a woman in black scrubs is restocking packages into a supply cabinet; my surgical resident is hunched over a computer searching for your brother's number. I'm fighting hard to maintain my composure.

I call my surgical partner, and when he answers, I immediately tear up. *Stop it*, I think, *you're a surgeon. You're supposed to be stoic.*

But my voice trembles as I tell him the news.

Our patient just died.

You.

*   *   *

It takes me two weeks to track down your brother, because you never gave us his number. When I finally reach him, I tell him all the details—the struggle of the surgery, the debut of your smile the morning after, the autopsy report that didn't cite a specific cause of death.

Your brother gives me some details in return. He tells me that you quit smoking cold turkey the day after I met you. From that day forward, you never touched your coffee-table pile of wrappers and tobacco (you rolled your own cigarettes to save money). They gathered a shroud of dust. When he asked you whether it was hard to quit, you just shrugged your shoulders and said you wanted the surgery.

You told him that you knew surgery had its risks, but you didn't care, because you didn't want to keep living the same old way without it. For over a year, you had been in and out of the hospital at least every other month with a full-blown bowel obstruction. It always meant another tube down your nose and another week without eating. You said you'd rather die than live that way.

I tell your brother how sorry I am that you died.

He says thanks anyway for trying to help you.

*   *   *

Almost a year and a half later, I'm on the Washington State Ferry. It's one of those perfect summer days that we reminisce about all winter long in the Pacific Northwest, when we're shivering for six months under a wet, grey blanket of sky. Today, everything is sparkling—the oiled feathers of seagulls flying around the dock, the blue expanse of Puget Sound, the far off snow caps topping the Olympic mountains. Nature has put on her finest attire, and everything feels alive.

I'm at the ferry's snack shop, eyeing all the goodies like a grown-up kid: hot dogs, hamburgers, pizza, popcorn, potato chips, candy, soda, ice cream bars. I'm paying for a soft pretzel when the intercom crackles.

"Shortly, the captain will be bringing the ferry to a complete stop in order to perform a brief memorial service. The engines will be turned off and the ferry will be completely still in the water for approximately five minutes."

In that instant, all the memories rush back—your belly full of snakes, your teeth, your smile, your grey face. Your brother, during our phone call, said he was hoping to arrange a memorial service for you on the ferry. He said the ferry was one of your favorite things. He said maybe I could come.

I don't know if your memorial service ever happened. If it did, I was never invited. I wouldn't blame your brother if he thought I might be too busy. Maybe, by the time he finally got a reservation, he thought I had already moved on from your death.

But, the truth is I haven't moved on, not completely. I still think of you every time I take the ferry, including today. Especially today.

I don't know if I'll ever "move on"—not now, a year and a half later, or even ten years from now. Every patient I've lost has created a wound. Even after the fresh wound heals over, the scar can be zinged unexpectedly—in your case, by a ferry ride, by someone sharing your first name, or by the rare sighting of cigarettes being hand-rolled.

The usually-smooth boat vibrates as the ferry protests its orders to halt. The other people in the galley continue on as if nothing out of the ordinary is happening, but I take a seat by myself and stare at the water, leaving my pretzel uneaten. Even though I know it isn't, it feels as if the memorial service being held upstairs is yours.

NIGHT SHIFT

ANEESH RAJMAIRA

My hands on your bare chest, I am your heart
Beating with incessant futility
Nameless, breathless, you are just some body

You were somebody, you had a story
Now we stand in a puddle of your blood
Slashing at your sides and slicing your throat

Moment of silence, less than a minute
Enough to acknowledge the loss of life
Enough. And it's over. Patients are waiting

Hours later, as if it didn't happen
I chat and laugh with your slashing surgeon
Outside the same room, outside your last room

I will remember you, I think

UNMASKING GRIEF

MARIA WOLFE

Almost twenty years have passed since that Friday in June during my fourth year of general surgery residency, yet I haven't forgotten the boy. Baby Jacob, I'll call him. He visits in the quiet spaces of my days, either alone or accompanied by another former patient. Once a day, once a week, once a month. Sometimes unprompted. Sometimes in response to an "I wonder…"

•   •   •

The lights in the neonatal intensive care unit were dim. A labyrinth of incubators filled the ward. However, after two previous rotations on the pediatric surgery service, I easily found my new patient. Baby Jacob slept in an open incubator not far from the nurses' station, undisturbed by the continuous soundtrack of monitoring devices and staff murmurs. At first glance he appeared healthy, pink-skinned and plump, incongruous among the tiny premature infants and critically ill babies.

Yet he was sick. And he was getting sicker. He wasn't even one day old.

The mother stood beside her son, her first-born child, gazing down at him. One fluid dripped into his IV and another into his orogastric tube. Wires connected him to the cardiac monitor above. With the clear plastic walls of the open incubator separating them, he must have seemed so far away, yet she closed the distance—her right hand caressed his bare leg in that universal, wordless language telling him that he was loved.

Untied, her yellow visitor gown slipped down her shoulders, bunching over her upper arms. The mother wore an oversized T-shirt and baggy pants, the comfortable going-home outfit that, weeks ago, she must have folded into her hospital bag along with a onesie and diapers and maybe a binkie for her son. After an uncomplicated spontaneous vaginal delivery at thirty-eight weeks of gestation, she'd had every expectation of bringing her son home.

Not long after his birth, a newborn screening test diagnosed the baby with an inborn error of urea metabolism, and he was urgently transported from a small outside hospital to the NICU of this top-ranked children's hospital. Though she hadn't known it, the mother was an asymptomatic carrier for an X-linked enzyme deficiency that she'd passed on to her son. In Baby Jacob, the disorder was causing a dangerous buildup of ammonia in his blood that could lead to severe neurologic injury or even death.

I introduced myself as the resident working with Dr. Aldrich, the pediatric surgery attending physician on call. "The metabolic team consulted us to place a hemodialysis catheter," I said. Despite optimal medical management, Baby Jacob's ammonia level was rising. To survive, he required urgent hemodialysis. The team wanted to start the treatment that same day.

The mother blinked at me, looking tired and dazed.

"The procedure will be performed in the operating room. Jacob will be asleep, under anesthesia." I pointed to his neck. "The catheter will go there."

She nodded.

"There are risks to any procedure, including this procedure." I recited the complications: bleeding, thrombosis, embolus, infection, pneumothorax, damage to adjacent structures, need for further procedures. These I could say without flinching. Before continuing, I took a deep breath, adding, "And death." The hard one, the irrevocable one, the one that shouldn't be associated with any infant or child. "There is a high risk of death."

Her hand stopped stroking Jacob's leg but didn't move away. She must have had so little contact with her son during this first day of his life. In the rush to transfer him to this hospital, maybe she hadn't even held him.

Death, I might have told the mother, was almost always included on the list of surgical complications. A standard disclosure. But, this time, Dr. Aldrich had told me, death was far more than just a slim possibility.

"The smallest hemodialysis catheter available is still too big for Jacob," I said. Dr. Aldrich had instructed me to emphasize the size discrepancy and its possible consequence. "Placing it could cause his death. Not doing the procedure is always an option." I shook my head. "But the metabolic team says he'll die without hemodialysis."

The mother agreed to the procedure. She took her hand from her son to sign the consent form fastened to the clipboard I held out to her.

*   *   *

The operating room was quiet. No music, no extraneous chatter. The cardiac monitor beeped out a rapid pulse as the ventilator sighed in and out.

The procedure went smoothly: placement of a hemodialysis catheter in the right internal jugular vein via venous cutdown. Under fluoroscopy, the catheter was advanced through a venotomy down the internal jugular vein to the superior vena cava. There was no room for error. The position of the catheter tip was verified at the atriocaval junction. While additional catheter length remained outside the tiny body, it couldn't be tunneled under the skin nor slid any farther inside.

"Looks fine," Dr. Aldrich said to the radiology tech. "Print out a hard copy of the image for the chart."

The incision was closed. The catheter was sutured in place. Its two stiff external limbs—one red, one blue—jutted from the baby's neck, their hubs towering over the top of his head. I'd never placed an HD catheter in a baby, but seeing how it dwarfed him worried me.

It must have worried Dr. Aldrich as well. He added layers of silk tape over the sterile dressing on the baby's skin, his neck too small to accommodate it all. "We can't let the catheter move." The two external limbs listed to the right until he taped them to the side of the baby's face.

"Okay to wake him?" the anesthesiologist asked.

Dr. Aldrich studied the baby. "We can't keep him intubated and sedated forever." He sighed. "Go ahead."

As soon as the endotracheal tube was removed, the baby cried. He twisted his head, left–right–left–right. His tiny fists flailed about as we transported him to the pediatric intensive care unit.

When we reached the PICU, he had already quieted down. After the PICU nurses had connected him to their monitors, his vital signs were stable.

"Once a final X-ray comes back and confirms the catheter placement," I told his nurse, "his hemodialysis can begin."

I returned to the OR to perform the final scheduled case of the evening with Dr. Aldrich.

•　　•　　•

"Jacob has a hemopericardium," Dr. Aldrich said as he shoved his hands into the sterile gloves that the scrub tech held out. As I prepped and draped the last patient, he'd run over to the PICU to check on Baby Jacob and the X-ray. "The cardiothoracic team was consulted."

My mouth dropped open behind my mask. No.

"The parents decided against surgery," he added.

The catheter had injured the blood vessel or maybe his heart. I don't know when it had happened but, at some point after the intraoperative X-ray, the device had shifted, maybe just a few millimeters, maybe less. Perhaps when suturing the catheter in place. Or when securing it with tape. Or when his head turned from side to side. Or when... Or when... Or when...

I had told the mother there was a high risk of death. Yet, somehow, I hadn't believed it myself. I had not expected the baby to die.

A one-day-old infant, dead. Dammit. Goddammit. I wanted to howl.

As we operated, Dr. Aldrich didn't mention the death. If he thought of the baby, he didn't show it.

But my chest hurt. Breathing was difficult. Still, I finished this last case. I tried to be like Dr. Aldrich: calm and professional. But, beneath my gown and mask, no one could see that my heart was breaking.

No one in medical school or my general surgery residency program taught me how to manage my feelings after a patient death. There was no class or seminar. Emotions were never discussed or acknowledged. The busy days and perpetual fatigue discouraged deep contemplation. Shoulders were shrugged; dark quips were exchanged. I learned to cope in silence by necessity—expressing grief was shameful, a sign of weakness that, in a surgeon, must be expunged. Be strong or else were the unvoiced options the culture offered. The or else was to be othered, to be less than. As an introverted female surgeon, I already felt apart. I donned a literal mask and a figurative mask to try to fit in.

So I'd learned to swallow my sadness. When adult patients died—not a lot, still too many—on the OR table, in the intensive care unit, on the patient wards, I brought the emotion home and sat with it privately before moving on.

The death of a pediatric patient, though? After three pediatric surgery rotations, I recalled only one other: a seven-year-old boy whom I'd worked up for a re-operative cardiac surgery for a congenital heart defect. Pikachu was his favorite Pokémon, and he scoffed at my choice: "All the girls like Jigglypuff." He didn't survive his surgery, I learned days later. The cardiothoracic fellow told me, blunt and detached, "There was too much scar tissue. I accidentally cut through his heart."

I had grieved for that little boy who loved Pikachu, but my sadness had come from a distance.

And then Baby Jacob died. This was different. Though I was just the resident, he had been under my care. His death was too close. How could I not feel it?

* * *

Only later, after I locked the door to the call room behind me, did my sternum open and the shards scatter, shatter. Little whimpers slipped past my clenched throat, struggling to hold the noises in as they fought to burst out. I didn't want to cry—that wasn't what surgeons did. I leaned against the wall. No. I sat on the bed. No. I dropped onto my hands and knees on the floor. And, as if an obstruction

20

had been relieved, I sobbed as I had never sobbed before. The pain was too much. Between cries, there was barely enough time to breathe.

The entirety of the tragedy overwhelmed me. I cried for the newborn baby who died. I cried for the young mother who lost her son. And, just a little, I cried for me.

Another general surgery resident heard me and knocked on the call room door until I finally let her in. "Are you okay?" Katie asked, closing the door behind her.

I didn't want anyone to see me like this, raw and hurting. I didn't want to talk about what had happened. But maybe, after three years of residency, she could comprehend the loss. I forced out the words to tell Katie about Baby Jacob.

"And Dr. Aldrich blames *you?*" Her tone was incredulous.

"No. Why would he?" I found a tissue and blew my nose. "It wasn't my fault."

Katie looked confused. "Well, then?" She gestured at me, at my red eyes, tear-streaked face, and runny nose. "What's wrong?"

"A baby *died*." I shook my head—I'd never seen Katie emotionally stumble after a patient death. Maybe she hid it better than I did; maybe it didn't bother her at all. If she couldn't understand my grief, I couldn't explain.

•   •   •

Mortality and Morbidity rounds for all the general surgery services took place on Wednesday mornings. For pediatric surgery, the fellow usually presented our complications from the past week.

But the fellow pulled me aside after Tuesday morning rounds. "You should present the case tomorrow morning."

As a resident, I was accustomed to answering "Yes" or "Of course." This time I said, "No." I would have discussed any other patient death, but not this one. "Absolutely not." Even days after the death, I couldn't talk about what had happened, not without a struggle to maintain my composure.

M and M was for reviewing what had gone wrong. I already understood the problem: a critically ill newborn needed a hemodialysis catheter, but, as Dr. Aldrich said, the appropriate size wasn't available. I didn't want to hear the recriminations: the whys, the whats, the hows. What would that accomplish? My guilt and self-doubt festered without the attendings' questions providing additional fuel.

What I needed was support. A kind word, even one, to let me know I wasn't alone. That it was okay to feel like this. I didn't get that. Not from Dr. Aldrich, Katie, or the fellow. It wasn't part of the culture. I knew that, and still, I wanted it.

The fellow didn't insist. I must have been too adamant in my refusal, and I had never refused anything before.

When the fellow stepped up to the podium on Wednesday morning to present, I left the room. Standing in the hallway, I breathed—in, out, in, out—until the sadness went away and I could return.

For a year or two, when the memory of Baby Jacob was new and scalpel-sharp, I avoided revisiting that awful Friday in June. But time has dulled its cutting edges and granted me some perspective. I look back and understand that my grief had been necessary. Unavoidable, even. A newborn had died that day, and I won't apologize for being a surgeon who cried.

THE FORMULA FOR WHOLENESS
KATHERINE DIBELLA SELUJA

The shape of his head was a pyramid,
a pyramid turned upside down.
His chin the pointed capstone
widening slowly into granite cheekbone
expanding further to the massive base.

Hector was born with only a brainstem
and miles of space and fluid
where the rest of his brain should have been.
I wanted to fill that space, all I could do was hold him.
Wrapped in cotton blankets, faded pink and blue stripes
the pink and blue of his veins more visible every day.

Some ancient impulse directed his tongue to grope and reach
for nurse's hand, blanket's edge, plastic tubing
that randomly brushed his face.
He gazed with protruding eyes at dark linoleum floors,
bright fluorescent lights,
late night radio on the shelf above his bassinet.

Each nurse took their turn with Hector,
each one sure that she could offer the cure
for space-where-brain-should-be.

And if not, then a mumbled Hindu prayer,
a leather pouch of Jamaican curry,
woven cross of fresh green palm.

His fontanel began to bulge.
I counted his irregular pulse there, in the little domed tent
that swelled at the top of his head.

He lost his will to suck, we lost one more way to soothe him.
And then it was only quiet and nurse's arms
and faded pink and blue,
a stone from Medjugorje, a string of ivory beads.

The prayer card with the bleeding-heart bursting
under a crown of thorns was tucked behind his bassinet
on the day I came to work and he was gone.

AND NOW I KNOW I WILL NEVER

KATHERINE DIBELLA SELUJA

pick up the scalpel. No one will
post my glove size
on the callboard by my name. I will never
observe the familiar tremor of my hand before I begin. I won't
feel the ease of subcutaneous tissue, the tension of edema.
It won't matter that my wrists are thin and my grasp is strong, no one
will answer my call for suction. I will never say: *I need a #10 blade now.*
Will never be blood-splattered and in fat up to my elbows. Won't slice
a ureter or nick an artery, pick up a bladder or relocate
a kidney. I will never stand
for twelve hours sweating under hot lights. I won't pull off
my blue scrub hat, break the sterile field, push backwards
through the door; walk slowly to a waiting room and wipe my face
before telling the family: I did everything I could.

TOUGH HAND
RICHARD MORAND

Leaning on the door of Trauma Bay 1, I survey the remains of my latest failure. The story is told in the bloody and jumbled instrument trays, monitors now silent and dark. In the center of the room sits a gurney covered with a white sheet and an unmistakable human form. Blood radiates outward on the sheet like ruined rose petals. On the floor maroon swatches catch patterned footprints here and there, like those of a hiker tracking through mud rather than this path through a man's essence.

I would have been a terrible gambler. I've been told a thousand times that I save far more than I lose, but it is an empty platitude. I have always agonized over losses far more than the satisfaction of any wins. Las Vegas would not want me.

John Doe 57 rolled in as so many before. "Hispanic male, mid-twenties, multiple stab wounds to the chest, no palpable blood pressure," the EMT said. Typical 3 a.m. patient. My team pounced. I was the trauma attending responsible for this enthusiastic and optimistic crew. Lines going, blood running, chest compressions and ventilation proceeding—all was fine. Blood poured from the left chest, and I knew what must come next.

I called for the chest tray, a command that assured every nearby provider would soon cram the room to watch that most invasive of procedures: thoracotomy. I can always feel their gaze like a heat lamp on my back when this call is made.

I splashed betadine and made the long left chest incision, spreading the ribs and gazing into a cavity no person should ever see. Upon opening the pericardium, the weakly pulsing heart was more grey than red, with a visible wound. One quick suture and the hole was sealed. John Doe 57's heart filled, and I thought I saw it pink up a bit, or was that just hope? The heart still beat rapidly, but as I helped its compression, I could tell that the muscle had lost its vitality. We soldiered on, shocking, replenishing blood, breathing for him, but it was all in vain. Eventually, I knew that as the lead, I must make the fateful call—03:44, time of death. Faster than the room had filled, team members slid away; nothing more to see here.

Now the room is silent as if nothing at all occurred. I stand watching the red stain forming on the pristine white sheet, mocking me in my failure. I trained at excellent institutions, survived residency, served in combat, and now, here at a Level I trauma center, with every possible medical tool at my disposal, I could not save this life. This injury, this particular injury, always has, and forever will, haunt my dreams. The hubris to think that I could be the difference, that I am better than those who came before me, was answered tonight, as it has been before, by this deserved slap in the face.

I absorb the charged silence; my mind wanders back to my third year of medical school. I was doing well, a moderate prodigy of the medical department. I was ready for every conference, every patient, well read and well prepared, until that fateful day.

I got the call late at night from my brother Pete. Our youngest brother Joe had been stabbed in the chest by the angry ex-husband of Joe's girlfriend. Joe made it to the hospital there in central Massachusetts, even made it alive to the operating room. The surgeon did not save him. Joe died on the table, only twenty-one years old.

Floating as if in a dream through the wake, funeral, and family obligations, I refused to meet or talk to the surgeon who attended Joe—that incompetent, probably poorly trained and ill-prepared joke of a surgeon. I would not have been able to account for my actions or words if I confronted him.

My return to medical school found me completely changed. I concentrated on surgery, canceled all my applications for medical residency, and quickly reapplied in general surgery. The life that followed—residency, Navy duty, combat surgery, and trauma training—led me to this doorway tonight. I was determined that I would right the wrong of the failings of my brother's incompetent surgeon. I would prove to the world and myself that death was not pre-ordained. It just took the proper education, dedication, training, and experience to prevent twenty-one-year-old boys from dying of wounds that had no right to kill them.

The truth was that I had all of this requisite preparation and more. I had the experience and now even the advantage of the best equipment that a Southern California major Level I trauma center could offer. Still, a twenty-something man lay dead on my gurney, just as dead as my brother had been at a small community hospital, somewhere in central Massachusetts. I think about that other surgeon now, as I have so many times in the past few years, and I am embarrassed.

I see a tired man in night's witching hours, answering the call and rushing into a hospital ill-equipped to handle the level of injury my brother represented. He probably had the same anxiety I have walking to the trauma bay as he drove into his emergency room. He called in the operating room crew—they wouldn't be on-site like they are here. Same with the anesthesia team. He had large bore IVs going, hung blood, and with whatever staff was available, ran for the operating room.

Joe's surgeon washed quickly and burst into the room, nauseated at the enormity of the task he must face virtually alone. I get this same feeling, even with my multitude of nurses, techs, residents, students, and frankly more people than I can ever use effectively. He opened the chest, made the repair as best he could. However, the pathology report would say that Joe died on that table of an air embolism, a sentence that would label that surgeon as a failure in my eyes for years, but no longer.

A surge of guilt rises in my throat. Guilt for my failure tonight, but more than that, guilt for my years of unjust judgment of Joe's surgeon. I have walked in his shoes many times, and the loss of each John Doe revives the horror and pain now binding me to that surgeon of many years ago. What right do I have to think that he did anything but his very best? What do I know of his training, experience, or dedication? He might have been good, better than I am, but he was not perfect or all-powerful. Neither am I.

I sometimes wish I could go back in time and have a coffee with this surgeon, this man. I would tell him that I know he did his best. I would say to him that even with all the tools in the world, the best staff right on-site, immediately available operating rooms, every possible blood product, in unlimited amounts, it would not have mattered. Neither of us is God, I would tell him. Sometimes the story has been determined; we are in the story, but we do not write it.

I would apologize to him for my years of scorn and humbly ask for his forgiveness. In my dreams, he shakes my hand. We do not speak, but our eyes meet, and we share an understanding of the fragile precipice each of us balances on every day. Joe's surgeon died years ago, so I will never be able to ask his forgiveness or give him mine. It is a regret that will always haunt me.

The bloody stain on the sheet spreads out, marking the time that moves on after death.

My reverie is interrupted by the orderlies. "Hey, Doc, we gotta take this guy to the morgue and get ready for the next one," they say, and, "Tough night, Doc, but you done good; you save a lot more than you lose, you know." That phrase again. I am learning to really hate it. It's the blackjack dealer saying, "Oh, tough hand, boss. Play again?"

I don't want to play again. Even if I win the next five hands, the one I lose will more than cancel it out. The gurney passes, and I slowly walk the quiet halls of the darkened hospital. I head to the nursery, often the place I gravitate to on nights like this. I look through the glass at the tiny faces swaddled in blankets, all pink and squished. White, Hispanic, Black, they all look pretty similar, and I like that. I just want to observe life; I want to see hope and promise and safety. Tonight it is hard to see.

My beeper goes off: "Code trauma major! Code trauma major!" it screams. I start walking briskly, but not running, back to Trauma Bay 1. My professors always said, "Walk, don't run. Center your mind and enter with confidence and purpose. Those around you will be looking to you for strength." What if I don't have it?

My crew of residents flies by me to prepare for arrival, yelling, "Let's go, boss! Isn't this great? A chance to cut is a chance to cure!"

A chance to cure. Perhaps, but it is also a chance to be faced once again with fear and reality. Yet I do walk in, make my best attempt at a smile, and take the report. "Gunshot wound to the abdomen, female, BP 90 over palp, two large-bore in place, intubated. Arrival by chopper, three minutes." I move to the head of the now new gurney; the room is sparkling clean, as if by magic; monitors are humming, new trays everywhere, my crew standing ready. I take a deep breath and silently ask, as I have so many times these past few years, "Hey there, Joe's surgeon, you with me on this one?" The door crashes open, and the cards are dealt again.

ELEGY IN AN O.R. LOCKER ROOM
DANIEL J. WATERS

You are there
        behind the caps and masks
          You are
              present in this
              empty space

You are not the work
        that will kill me
          You are
              the worry

You are not the decision
        that keeps me awake
          You are
              the doubt

You are not the thousand
        things that went right
          You are
              the one that
              went wrong

You are not the smiles
        that haunt me
          You are
              the tears

You are not the successes
        that follow me
           You are
                the failures

You are not the survivors
        who thank me
           You are
                the dead
                I visit

In this imaginary churchyard
        where I kneel
           and pray for
                forgiveness

ADMISSION

The curtain is symbolic of lack, of impotency, of inability to protect or hide—body, voice, illness, truth. What do we try to keep behind the curtain? How does the curtain fail us? What do we need that the curtain cannot provide?

Discuss whether you consider this piece poetry or prose. Notice the use of repetition and discuss its effect. Consider the relationship between form and meaning in this work and discuss your impressions. Describe what Hu may have intended by beginning and ending the piece with a dash.

⚒ *Write about what isn't enough.*

SILENT INTERCESSION

"But in simply uttering her name, I unlocked the door to the hidden place where I sequester grief when it refuses to behave." What cultural expectations do we have about how grief should behave? Among the genders? In medicine? What interpretations and judgments do we make about ourselves and others when grief fails to behave as we expect? What do you think is the adaptive purpose or function of grief?

The narrator's inability to articulate her prayer in this one moment is an accumulation of the blows of grief she has absorbed and its impact on her faith. How does Sato manipulate time in this piece to explore those different griefs? What in the end is her prayer?

⚒ *Write about holding back or letting go.*

HELPING YOU

Kantola addresses the patient directly as "you" in this piece. What would change if the perspective were third-person, talking about the patient rather than to him? What effect does the use of "you" have on your sense of the narrator's relationship with the patient? On your identification with the patient?

The narrator states, "Yes, I can probably help you, and helping you is probably going to cost me." What are the costs and burdens of helping? Why do we accept them?

After surgery, before the patient dies, the narrator considers the case a success. Discuss how, despite the fact that the patient died, the case could still be considered a success.

⚒ *Write about risk.*

NIGHT SHIFT

"Nameless, breathless, you are just some body / You were somebody, you had a story." At what moment does somebody become just some body? What are the risks to the healthcare professional of somebody? Some body?

Discuss the use of punctuation, or lack thereof, in this poem. What do you perceive were Rajmaira's intentions? Discuss the possibilities of meaning in the title.

🖎 *Write about some body.*

UNMASKING GRIEF

"Shoulders were shrugged; dark quips were exchanged. I learned to cope in silence by necessity—expressing grief was shameful, a sign of weakness that, in a surgeon, must be expunged. Be strong or else were the unvoiced options the culture offered. The *or else* was to be othered, to be less than." Connect Wolfe's statement with Sato's expectations of grief's behavior. What would a shift in the culture look like? How might this kind of shift create tension within the healthcare system? Talk about when it is necessary and appropriate to mask grief and when it isn't.

In both "Unmasking Grief" and "Silent Intercession," the narrators describe unstoppable tears. Examine the imagery used in the two scenes of emotional release. Compare and comment on the different reactions each narrator receives from those who witness this outpouring.

🖎 *Write about masking or unmasking.*

THE FORMULA FOR WHOLENESS

Seluja uses powerful allusions and images in this poem—some ancient and sacred, some modern. Which are most memorable to you and why? What is the relationship between these images and cure? What is the relationship between cure and wholeness?

🖎 *Write about a sacred image.*

AND NOW I KNOW I WILL NEVER

Discuss the language of negation in Seluja's poem. Speculate about why the narrator "will never." Do you perceive this to be a poem of longing or protest? Give evidence for your response.

🖎 *Begin with "I will never..."*

TOUGH HAND

One theme developed in "Tough Hand" is the effect of time and age on one's perspective about the ability to control patient outcomes. Identify young characters in this story. How does Morand use their voices and demeanor to foil or contrast his mature perspective?

Referring to the healthcare professional, in this case the surgeon, Morand writes, "Sometimes the story has been determined. We are in the story, but we do not write it." To what extent do you think this is or isn't true? Discuss who you aspire to be in your patient's story.

✎ *Write from the perspective of someone you need to forgive.*

ELEGY IN AN O.R. LOCKER ROOM

Anaphora is a repetition of a word or words at the beginning of successive lines or stanzas in a poem. Discuss the power of anaphora in this poem. How does that repetition mimic the space of the locker room? What is the effect of breaking the pattern in the final stanza?

How does this poem speak to other pieces in this section?

✎ *Write about what happens in the locker room or breakroom.*

SECTION TWO

LIKE ANY GOOD TRICK

DANIEL BECKER

All those statues of saints draped in rosary
and gathered at the bedside?
They're praying for enough pain here and now

to qualify for early and eternal redemption.
Or so explains a son who trusts his mom
to suffer as long and hard as she needs to.

What do I know? Who should I trust?
I have to trust the sons and daughters.
At some point a reflex hammer appears in my hand,

the cheap kind that looks like a rubber tomahawk
and without a lot of practice lacks the angular momentum
that testing deep tendon reflexes requires.

I spin it on my index finger.
I can do that with my eyes closed.
I can do that walking down the hall and checking my to-do list.

I'm a professional. That's one of my earliest tricks.
Like any good trick, it's harder than it looks.
I can also juggle causes and effects, mistakes and regrets.

SPIDER-MAN
ANNA-LEILA WILLIAMS

The woman arrived screaming. A deep primal scream. Time stalled as our senses shifted from aural to visual, from the desperate animal cry to the red and blue Spider-Man costume spilling from her arms. Time sputtered when, in quick succession, we saw the costume's red drip to the floor and then, by her elbow—a boy's head. Someone bellowed, "Pedi Code! Pedi Trauma!"

Time accelerated as we spun the intricate and precise choreography of trauma response team. Tiny Spider-Man, without pulse or breath, lay center stage. The woman-we-assumed-to-be-Mom stood just beyond the curtain, telling their story.

My son has a cold, so I decided to drive him to trick-or-treat. We hadn't gone far. I...I wasn't going fast. I didn't see anything, but I...I heard...my God, I felt the thud! I stopped the car and found Spider-Man... lying in the road. He...he must have run in front of my car. I scooped him up, put him in the backseat and drove here....No, I don't know his name or age. My son is in the car; he might know. He's going to be okay, right? Please, please...he has to be okay.

We heard the nurse take the woman-we-assumed-to-be-Mom-who-was-actually-the-driver-of-the-vehicle-that-hit-Spider-Man to an exam room to wait for the police.

Not long after, that same nurse stood by the curtain with Spider-Man's parents. She guided them to hold their son's feet while, inches away, we tried to push life back into his body.

I don't remember his name. I don't ache on his birthday or feel his phantom kiss on my cheek. I'm not brought to my knees by his favorite color, Dr. Seuss books, spaghetti, or strawberry ice cream. I don't mourn when I see UNO cards, Lego blocks, rubber dinosaurs, or sneakers that light up with every step. I don't weep at the smell of mud or freshly shampooed hair.

I'm not his mom or his auntie, and yet, I cared for him. Decades ago, I felt his ribs bend under my weight as I tried to coax his heart to beat. And every October, I look for him amid the tiny tricksters that ring my doorbell.

By now, he would be one of the handsome dads, hanging back on the sidewalk, reminding his own little superhero to say thank you.

A RAPID DECLINE
THOM SCHWARZ

At nine-thirty on a muggy, late summer night, Chuck, the adult son of my patient Charles, called to ask questions about his father's failing condition. "He's slipping away," he said, his voice slack with fatigue and resignation.

"I hate to bother you," he offered, "but I just need to be sure."

"Be right there," I replied.

The half-hour drive to their home was quiet, uneventful. The next day was the first day of the new school year. The country lanes would be busy with yellow buses, filled with wide-eyed, fresh-faced schoolchildren. Now the roads were empty, everyone home from one last trip to the mall, tucked in early. As I drove I reviewed what I knew about the patient and his family, the pertinent facts. Seventy-two years old. Lung cancer. A widower, his wife passed less than a year ago. He had been rapidly declining the past few days. Chuck, who was staying with him for the time being, had begun giving his father lorazepam for his terminal restlessness and a fast-acting liquid morphine solution to keep him comfortable. Now, Charles was actively dying.

Charles' singlewide trailer was squeezed between two others on the loop road around the pond where two dozen more crowded close like giant loaves of bread. Unremarkable and utterly plain on the outside, the trailer was spotlessly clean and surprisingly cozy inside. The kitchen appliances were twenty years old but hummed stolidly. The counters were empty, surprisingly—no piles of unopened bills, no supermarket flyers or the flotsam and jetsam of a busy life recently rendered pointless by the loss of a lifelong mate. There was a dim, welcoming light by the front door. A green shaded pendant lamp hung over the kitchen table, and a gentle nightlight beckoned from the bedroom at the end of the narrow hall. The President of the United States was talking sincerely on the television in the living room, although no one in this home was paying attention. He was aural wallpaper.

Before I listened to Charles's lungs, I asked Chuck to shut off the TV to make it easier to auscultate his father's nearly absent breath sounds. In the narrow living room, Chuck sat next to his aunt, Muriel. She'd come to clean, cook, and care for her baby brother, the dying Charles of Bourdette County, New York.

"I really don't think there's any more you, or anybody, can do for my father, but I just wanted to make sure that we're doing all we can to keep him comfortable," Chuck said. He smiled gently, a glint of tears in his eyes. I might have mistaken that for a happy twinkle, if it weren't for the wet crackle of his father's cough, the drone of the oxygen concentrator, and the burbling of its humidifier, harbingers of why I was visiting.

On the drive home I was not alone anymore. I felt Charles with me, and I was certain he would not live out the night. Had I told his son everything he needed to know? The timing and proper use of the medications? The difference between Ativan to quiet his father's agitation and atropine to dry the respiratory secretions trying to drown him? How to accurately draw up a miniscule dose of morphine in an eyedropper? And that I'll return with a urinary catheter to keep him dry and comfortable when he can no longer pee? "Thanks, but no thanks, no catheter. He's proud. He's still strong," Chuck had said. "I can help him use the urinal." *Not for long*, I'd thought.

At three-thirty in the morning, the pager on my bedside table squealed its sleep-piercing tone. I fumbled in the dark and strangled its off button. I knew it requested a return call to Chuck. My knowing this was beyond the mere anticipation that kept my brain twenty percent awake. How is this intuition born? Experience? Shared anxiety? I padded quietly through my kitchen trying not to wake the three dogs stretched out on the cool linoleum floor. They never hear my beeper.

Seated at my desk, I returned Chuck's call. We spoke in quiet voices, man to man. He was grateful; I was sorry. He said there was froth coming from his father's nose and mouth. I knew just what that would look like, could see it as if he was right in front me.

"What should I do?" he asked. "This is all new to us," he added apologetically. *No one gets to practice this beforehand*, I thought. No one would want to, even if they could.

"Your father is declining very quickly," I said sadly. As his father lay fading, I felt my own presence beside them there in the trailer.

"How long do you think he has? I know you can't know for sure, but in your experience?"

That's the one question families always ask, I explained, the one question patients never ask, and the one question I can't answer. "I don't think it'll be long. I suspect very soon." I overstated the obvious to make sure he wasn't missing my message in the thrall of his well-concealed grief.

"Give him the atropine now," I suggested.

"The eye drops?" he asked.

"Yes, four drops in the corner of his mouth. And a full measure of the morphine every two hours." *That is, if he holds on another two hours*, I thought.

Hanging up the phone felt like Chuck walking me to the door of the trailer. Letting me go. There was nothing more to say.

Back at my desk, I put down the receiver. When I looked up, there sat Charles at the table behind a berm of coffee cups, unfolded laundry, and a mound of magazines and unopened mail. His breathing was shallow and muffled by the froth of saliva like sea foam blowing before a storm. My dogs slept soundly on the cool floor. Even Blue, the Great Dane whose nights are often fitful with puppy dreams was still as stone. They couldn't see Charles; only I could as he shifted silently on his chair and stared at me.

An hour later Charles was gone. The pager's squeal didn't wake me; I choked it off as it began to hum. I returned Chuck's call to learn what I already knew Chuck wouldn't be able to bring himself to say. Not that word, not yet. Maybe later today, but not this soon.

At 5 a.m. I returned to Charles's trailer. Chuck and Muriel sat on the edge of the love seat, holding coffee mugs with both hands for the warmth. They mumbled about a distant brother already on his way, Charles's last meal of canned tomato soup, and how he had chosen his own casket last week. "He was a carpenter, you know," Chuck informed me. "The lady at the funeral home could tell he didn't like her caskets. She had said, 'You're a carpenter, why don't you build your own?' But he didn't have the strength anymore."

The September sun was rising red over the ancient Taconic hills when I turned into my driveway. The dogs were awake, grinning and panting urgently at me over the half-open Dutch door. Behind them my kitchen was empty. Upstairs, my son's and daughter's beds have been empty for months; they are in college and traveling, respectively. No more waiting for the yellow school bus at the end of the driveway. My wife's car was gone; she'd left for work. The dew on the grass caught the light through the maple trees. They were just beginning to turn. I turned off the night light on my way through the kitchen, dropped my dew-wet shoes by the bed, and lay down, still in my clothes. The sheets on my wife's side were as ruffled as a stormy sea. She doesn't sleep well when I am out seeing patients all night. Behind my eyes there is pain like guncotton, running down behind my ears to my neck. But I can sleep now, finally. I'm alone again.

MEDICINE: A HAUNTING
CHRISTOPHER BLAKE

Was that a footfall on the step? No. I'm imagining things, but still my heart is pounding as I lie in bed. "I don't believe in ghosts," I tell myself.

"Is that right?" asks the voice in my head. "So who switched on the kitchen light at midnight on an island occupied by you and your dog?"

"Possibly I left the light on," I think.

"The light flicking on is what woke you. As you well know."

Brigus growls and shakes herself awake as I shrug on a sweater.

"Such a great idea you had," says the voice. "Coming alone to the island in the foggy, dead-end of fall to escape the hospital and write."

I haven't seen another human in a week, other than the hazy, crooked form of a fisherman trolling the mist. I haven't turned on the television, checked the Internet, or listened to the radio. The world could have fallen to apocalypse and now some mutant form might lurk across the kitchen curtain.

Brigus pushes her way through the drape and keeps growling. The only weapon around is a heavy flashlight I heft against my palm. I creep to the curtain, imagining facing a man with a hunting rifle, imagining seeing...something. But I step through and there's nothing; just the living room lamp, casting its monstrous shadows, and me, shivering in the inadequate glow.

•   •   •

The human mind fears entropy. It seeks order. It seeks patterns where there are none because patterns mean information, the difference between life and death.

The human mind cannot brook uncertainty. There is a reason that, as a boy, my mind invented terrors in the shape of the kitchen cupboard. Darkness is the ultimate uncertainty and, left alone, imagination will populate it with every possible horror.

At night you may say you don't believe in ghosts but your nerves know otherwise. Your brain will dilate your pupils, set your heart thudding, leave you sweating at the sound of an unseen step. Your brain is trying to keep you alive. Your mind is merely trying to stay sane.

•   •   •

It takes time to drift off but eventually exhaustion fades into sleep and then morning light is waking me. A new day has come to silence the voice insisting on terror.

I experiment with the rogue lamp's knob. It's loose. Even the tread of a mouse would be enough to switch it on and awaken a grown man to monsters. Mystery solved. Or so I tell myself.

I drink tea and write with the dog curled at my feet. I put on rainwear and walk her amidst the muted leaves, the soil smelling of damp iron. A single boat passes. I'm unsure if it's the fisherman from before.

Dusk falls and I light the woodstove and stoke it until I'm sweating. I barbeque dinner and watch the stars turn on while the dog crashes through the forest, barking at something invisible. In the distance, wolves howl back and I imagine this place when the glaciers steamrolled everything. I think of the winter I was here. A deer stood frozen on the ice like a totem, then shot off into nothing. It is strange how lonely the closest place I have to home can be.

I let the fire burn down and check the locks before climbing into bed.

"Not that they would stop anyone," says the voice.

I'm being ridiculous. I'm perfectly safe. Anyone approaching has to come over water and I'd hear feet tramping through forest long before anything got to me.

"But you wouldn't hear a ghost," says the voice.

"Then it's good they don't exist."

"Of course they don't," the voice sneers.

It takes a long time but I do sleep. I do sleep.

·　　·　　·

A different night. Another haunting. In the ER, a woman is dying: my age, head-on collision. Really, she's dead before the team even gets to work but it takes nearly an hour before they stop compressions and accept what entropy has done, the destruction wrought upon this person, upon the spirit of her family.

But there's a shift to finish and I finish it, thinking less of the mangled body than of the paramedic who'd brought her in, how he'd collapsed in tears when the time of death was called. Maybe he has a daughter. Maybe he's lost someone like this.

When I get home it's late. I slip into bed and stare at the ceiling. In palliative care, I'm used to death. The work I do—people ask, *My god, how can you bear it? How can you stand such loss?* But it doesn't usually affect me. Not like this. In my work there's some order, some predictability. It's nothing at all like walking into the room of a dead woman's family and shattering their world.

"Maybe you could have saved her," says the voice.

CHRISTOPHER BLAKE | *MEDICINE: A HAUNTING*

"No," I think. "She was dead before she came in."

"Okay, fine, not her. What about the others who died on your watch?"

"Listen, I did everything I could—"

"But not enough."

I don't respond and neither does the voice. It's made its point. Headlights strafe the blinds, punctuating the wall with staccato fluorescence. The air conditioner clicks off, then on again. The alarm clock ticks off minutes in red like teacher's ink.

HAIR CLIPS FOR ESMA

LILA FLAVIN

I pressed my body into the wall as they wheeled her past. The child's feet were flopped to the side, pudgy thighs sticking out from under tangled sheets. A black belt around her waist held her down to the stretcher. I followed them into the room.

A nurse stuck a long needle into the crook of her arm and I flinched. I hadn't learned to hold my expressions steady when we hurt our patients. The chubby toddler didn't move. She didn't cry as the syringe filled with blood.

"She's febrile to 104," the resident said. "She's tachy too." He jammed at the mousepad, then flicked the IV bag, hoping it would make the medication release faster. He checked her blood pressure, tightening the cuff around her rolls of fat. "She's in septic shock," he said.

I backed further into the corner of the room. I wanted to be helpful, to do something to make her lips get their color back, but I was a medical student and lacked the training. After a while, the resident looked up, remembered I was there and told me it was late, that I should go home. When I didn't move, he said: "She'll be alright. See you tomorrow." Her lips were still gray.

As I rode the elevator down to the lobby, I held my pocket-sized guide to pediatric medicine to my chest. I walked out of the hospital into the cold winter night, marveling at how the world moved on no matter what terrors happened inside.

The next morning when I came in, I put on the gloves, the gown that reached my ankles, and the mask, then turned the knob on the door. Her crib was in the center, with wires connecting her to blinking monitors and bags of fluids hanging from poles. Coarse pink curtains grazed the linoleum floor. Other than a couch pushed into one corner, the room was empty—no traces of any visitors at all.

I walked towards the crib and leaned my shoulders against the high bars. Suspended from the crib was a collection of dangling toys, a squishy yellow ball and a hard blue bunny. I looked over the bars at the child, whom I'll call Esma, and saw her lips were pink and full now. Her ears were covered with downy hairs and pierced with diamond earrings, which I assumed were a gift from her parents. Esma's round cheeks looked yellow from the bright light. She had a c-shaped dimple on her chin.

I whispered her name through the bars. She turned slightly towards the sound, saliva pooling at the corner of her mouth. Her eyes tracked mine. I brought my hand to hers; her muscles were soft and underdeveloped. I pushed back the hospital wristband, rubbing my thumb against the backside of her hand. She didn't squeeze back. Her lips opened and closed without a sound.

Her hair was thick, covering the white pillowcase. I brought the stethoscope to her back. Her lungs sounded like crinkling tissue paper. I whispered as I examined her, telling her that her heart sounded strong, that I thought she had beautiful hair. Even though we were alone, and the door was closed, I was surprised by the gentleness in my voice. The role of caregiver was new to me and I was pleased that it was one that suited me. I had to remind myself to look at her oxygen saturation on the monitor before I left the room, to count her respirations by watching the rise and fall of her chest.

"How'd she look?" the resident asked later that morning.

"She looks so healthy," I said. "She looks like a normal kid."

He smiled. "No, I mean her lungs. How do they sound?"

"Oh, right. Yes, a lot of consolidation."

"The junkiest I've ever heard," he replied. "She would have been dead if she'd gotten here any later." He was angry about the night before. He listed his grievances: the staff at the facility had waited too long to call the ambulance, the EMTs hadn't given her enough fluids, the emergency department had messed up the antibiotics. He was angry that other people's mistakes had made her sick. But perhaps more so he was angry that it had fallen on him at the end of a long day, as he had been about to go home, to save her.

When I returned to her room the following morning, her hair was combed and pulled into pigtails using two scrunchies. I touched her hair and sparkles covered my gloved hand. I didn't know who had done her hair—not her parents, who lived far away and hadn't been able to visit often. I imagined that a person working overnight had slid the elastic off her wrist; maybe it belonged to her own child. Had she talked to Esma the way I did as she'd combed her hair?

I imagined that the two of us made up a twenty-four seven team. I watched out for Esma during the day, and while I slept, the night person took over talking to her, fixing her hair, wiping the spit off the side of her face. It seemed that everyone in the hospital was busy except for me. As a medical student, I rounded with the team in the morning and wrote one to two notes in the afternoon. That left me hours of time to sit behind the nurse's station, wander back and forth past Esma's room, occasionally drop in to see her.

Later that week, I gave a presentation to the team about Esma's genetic disorder. I stood outside Esma's door as I spoke to the attending, resident, and intern. I willed my hand not to shake as I read from the list of bullet points I'd prepared, words like leukodystrophy and peroxisomal dysfunction. I used medical terms to describe the severe genetic disorder that affected every organ in her body, especially her nervous system. It felt satisfying to intellectualize her disease, to talk about the organelles and enzymes of her body, instead of the ways she and her family had suffered because of it.

I hoped that Esma would begin to recognize me. I wanted her to turn her head when I walked in the room, squeeze back on my hand, maybe even smile, or coo. I knew it was impossible: her nerves lacked the ability to send messages to her muscles. Still, I waited for a sign that I was important to her. Or perhaps, I wanted something in this hospital, with its plastic wrapped syringes and professionally disinfected toys, to feel familiar to her.

My classmates and I had spent the first two years of medical school in the classroom, seated side by side, squinting at *PowerPoints*, or filling in bubbles on multiple choice tests, hoping we'd acquire enough percentage points to make it to the next step. At the beginning of our third year we came together, all two hundred of us, for a one-week intensive "boot camp." I was nervous, but I didn't stop grinning. Finally, I was going to wear my white coat every day and not just admire it each time I opened my closet. Until this point, my classmates and I had experienced everything together—every lecture, every test. Now we were splitting up to different hospitals and different specialty services all around the state. We wouldn't be together again until graduation.

When I met Esma, I was about halfway through my third year of medical school. I'd already made it through clinical rotations in psychiatry, obstetrics and gynecology, and surgery. The hospital was beginning to feel less foreign to me. I didn't have to google as many medical words or abbreviations during rounds. I rarely put my stethoscope on backwards. When a doctor asked me a question, my eyesight no longer blurred from panic. But even though I was improving, it wasn't until I was alone with my patients that I felt I could relax: we were both out of place in the hospital, and perhaps we saw that in each other.

Halfway through my pediatrics rotation, I had time off for break. Esma had been responding to the antibiotics: her fever had gone down and her chest X-ray looked clearer. I opened the door, heard the familiar beep of the medication drip. The midnight person had arranged Esma's hair so it was half up and tucked into a barrette. I made sure the door was shut, then I moved my mask to the side and kissed the girl's small forehead.

When I got home, I stuffed my dirty white coat in the hamper and told myself to leave the hospital behind. That night, I packed my suitcase and left for the airport early the next morning. I would meet my family in Bogota, and together we would fly to the coast. Once I arrived in Columbia, I stood in line at customs, kicking my duffel bag forward. It occurred to me that the last six months in the hospitals had felt like an extended study abroad experience, every month or so going to a new hospital, and a new specialty service, where I learned new acronyms, new ways of talking, new speeds of eating. I craved something familiar. I wanted to be home. I wanted to be with my classmates, the only people who knew exactly what I was going through. This trip felt like a bad idea, but it was too late to turn back.

A few days into the trip, I got sick, most likely from a virus I'd caught from one of the patients in the hospital. Each time I swallowed, I felt sharp prickles inside my throat. I had a fever and alternated between shivering and sweating on the hotel's smooth white sheets. I was angry that the hospital's viruses had followed me here, onto the plane, then into this new country. I pictured the resident, still at the hospital, eating dinner from a Styrofoam container, and then I felt guilty for feeling sorry for myself. He was still there and I had escaped.

I'd brought a spiral notebook with me on the trip. At boot camp they'd told us we were supposed to process, that we had to deal with what we were going through so we could come back refreshed for our patients. I flipped to an empty page. I didn't want to process. Processing was for people who didn't have fevers, who were rested and happy; but I wanted to feel better, so I followed the instructions.

I wrote with a dull pencil across the lined page: "It's not fair." I wrote it three times in a font somewhere between cursive and block. Below it I drew the shape of her face. It was a wide oval, a pointed triangle for the chin. I drew straight hair pulled into pigtails. Her eyes were closed in the drawing, placed too far up the forehead. The top line of her lips made a capital M. Her face was all symbol, those eyes, the ears, and the lips were the same ones I'd draw on every face since seventh grade. I was trying to pin her down, freeze her, make her stay the way I remembered her.

I kept the notebook beside me on the bed for a long time. The air conditioning was too strong, carpet thick and white in a way only hotels can maintain. I heard the sound of kids playing in the pool outside, the clang of dishes from the cafe. I felt alone. I had no words to describe how her situation, her isolation, lingered with me even on another continent. I couldn't call her my niece, my family friend, my cousin. As a medical student, I felt silly even calling her my patient. My patient.

My patient. It implied an ownership that I didn't feel ready for.

When I got to the hospital after break, I had a set of hair clips with me. I'd seen them dangling from a hook beside the grocery store checkout and dropped them in my basket. I planned to leave them in the crib for the midnight person to put in Esma's hair. I played with them in the pocket of my white coat on the elevator ride up.

I turned the knob on Esma's door. There was a woman sitting on the couch, clutching an iced coffee. There was a trio of yellow balloons above her head. At first, I thought this was Esma's mother; but then a small boy sat up in Esma's crib and yelled.

I went to the back room. "Did Esma leave?" I asked the resident. He was in between bites of a sesame bagel. There was a glob of cream cheese on his thumb and I waited to see where it would end up.

"You didn't know?" he said. "She died. When was it?" He scratched his head. "I think it was on a Saturday or Sunday. I remember because I was on."

"Wait, what? She died? Esma died?"

He nodded. He passed me the sign out with the names of the new patients.

I looked at the list, searching for her name. Could he be mistaken?

"I'm sorry," he said as I ran my finger down the page. "Esma wasn't a great learning case. I'll help you find a better one."

I looked up. I could tell he wanted to say more but I was glad when he didn't. That back room was a place where we shared our frustration, sometimes our anger, but never our sadness.

When I got home that night, I fell onto the couch. My partner asked how my day was and I shook my head. I cried while feeding myself forkfuls of pasta. I tried to tell my partner about Esma but all that came out were vague statements like, "It's so sad," or "It's not fair," or "She was so young." Eventually I did stop crying, not because the sadness had passed, but because there were things I had to do to get ready for the next day. Later that night, I put the hair clips in my dresser and shut the drawer.

The following week, I told my clerkship director that my first patient had died. I hadn't planned to tell her; it surprised me even as I said the words. Her office was warm, with plants lining the window sill and photos of children on the desk. Maybe I thought she could help me understand why I couldn't stop thinking about Esma's little hands. She looked at the place where I gripped the armchair. She scooted closer. "I guess we forget how involved you are as medical students," she said.

It's been three years since Esma died. I still think about Esma. I think about that moment when I first found out she was gone. I can still see that resident sitting at the table. I see his white coat on the back of the chair, his two pagers and stethoscope in a pile beside his elbow, the stubble on his chin, the bits of gray starting to peek out behind his ears. At first, I had been angry with him. What if he had said more? How might he have helped me to cope with that loss? That image of him would morph into one of me. I would be the one crouched at the table, hand on my chin, relaying to the medical student some adverse event as if giving the morning weather report. I feared that I would have no control over whether or not this transformation would happen to me.

I'm halfway through my intern year. Now when I think of that resident, all I can imagine saying is, "You have a hard job." I have a hard job.

When I look back at that drawing of Esma in my notebook, I am reminded of the little girl, but also of the younger version of me, of how much she wanted to hold on. I close the notebook, put it on the shelf, and get ready for another day.

TRAUMA BAY

SHANNON ARNTFIELD

Twenty-something ponytail,
wrinkled scrubs and racing heart
walk-runs empty halls to you

unbelted, ejected, back middle seat
burst windshield onto gravel where
you slid for thirty feet under
moonless black sky.
Led with your face.

They call it de-gloving when
the skin peels back
sheer force exposing
bone muscle fat like an anatomic drawing
but the textbook never showed the shards of glass or
stony dirt buried your length of hip to arm to cheek.

Primary survey, skip past the 'A'—
tube's down your throat—and pierce
a hole in your chest, blade
lets blood escape, space
your lungs need to breathe.
Take long graceful neck, cannulate
veins running to your heart,
fill the tank running low of
red fluid life.

You're wearing a black lace thong and
matching bra I have to cut and
I can't help
but think of what you hoped
when you got dressed tonight.

Secondary survey—look into your eyes, dark
fanning lashes frame
pupil, blown
on that one side, that doesn't respond to light,
as unflinching to this chaos
as you are and I'm not and I
start the medication to stop
swelling in your brain.

My tears come and I
have to look away. Your face
is not your face
and your black lace bra, it mocks us.

GRAVITY

PAIVI E. PITTMAN

It is the same day over and over. You just wish they seemed different. So you buy yourself whatever you can. Say to yourself whatever you can. The art of covering it up. The fact you wished you were somewhere else. The fact you wished you were someone else.

There is a pile of orders waiting to be made. Scrub up. Dress down. Go into the Clean Room. Mix the drugs and diluents until each label is done. Then go to the nursing stations with a cart full of IVs. The nurses will swear they needed them a half hour ago.

You never remember the patients' names. Not Mr. Russell in Room 337, but KCl in D5 ½ NS. Patients are not who they are but what drug they need.

Six East. ICU. Swipe your card to get in. The nurses seem busy. Intent. Your life lacks purpose. You know it. Maybe you have always known it. The pain follows you around like a mangy dog that wants to be fed. Walk down the hall to the med room. Bend down to put the IV bags into the refrigerator. Glance in the room across the hall.

That is when you notice her. Through the glass wall of the next room. It is hard to see her face, really. Bandages wrapped around her head. Blood soaked. Her chart indicates a single bullet to the brain.

See your reflection slightly as the light bounces off the glass. Her face. Then your face. Then her face again. Hear the echo play inside your head. Thoughts set up shop and demand a wage. What you need. What you still want. Out of this life or the next. Days go by. You think you can ignore the pain. You think you can ignore the wanting. But you cannot escape it.

She is not a label. She is not just another order to be made. She is a sign to remind you what can happen if you try to silence yourself. If you try to remain as you are. Stuck between being silent about the pain and letting the pain silence you.

We are both here—in reciprocal emergencies.

SHELF LIFE
HOWARD F. STEIN

For Seth Allcorn

Grocers talk of the shelf life
Of food in cans, jars, bottles, boxes.
I inspect plastic-wrapped
Cheese and bread for the first sign
Of putrid green mold.
Fresh meats and frozen fruits
All have labels on their wrap
That read Best Used by This Date—
When wholesome food turns to rot.
All my medicines
Come in bottles
Somewhere stamped
With an expiration date,
The moment white magic
Decays into black.
How much battery-life
Remains in these once-new
Alkaline AA cells I discover
Deep in my kitchen drawer
Years after I had placed them
There just in case?
In this sputtering body,
Worn down by how it lived,
Scars on the surface
Hint at sordid stories beneath
That had been cut out
Or repaired just in time.
Eventually I begin to wonder
How much shelf life I have left.

SURROUNDED

PAMELA A. MITCHELL

everywhere I look I am encircled

in the last few weeks two of us

laid aside our stethoscopes   and died

another two   are dying still

it is too much   coming home

now my dog   is crying

I suddenly know   it is written everywhere

the scrawl of death's trembling mark

I think of Karla

only next month   she was to fly to China to receive

a baby girl

we heard the code in Emergency

little did we know   it was one of our own

DISCUSSION AND PROMPTS

LIKE ANY GOOD TRICK

How would you describe the tone of this poem? Discuss the claim, "I'm a professional." What does that mean in the context of the poem? Discuss the metaphor of the reflex hammer. What is the role of reflexivity in medical practice? How does this connect to prayer? To trust?

> *Write about something that is harder than it looks.*

SPIDER-MAN

How is the speaker in Williams's story haunted? How does she differentiate her grief from that of the boy's family members? Is this differentiation necessary? Are there rules governing who gets to grieve and how?

Notice what Williams writes about time. "Time stalled…time sputtered…time accelerated…" How do trauma and grief affect our experiences of time, and why do you think this is so?

> *Write about something you don't remember.*

A RAPID DECLINE

In this story, Schwarz uses imaginative and fantastical elements to cross the physical boundaries of place and presence both before and after the patient's death: "They couldn't see Charles; only I could as he shifted silently on his chair and stared at me." Find other places in the text where this occurs. Discuss this transcendence of boundaries from various perspectives, such as spiritual, social, psychological, and even occupational.

> *Write about "being with."*

MEDICINE: A HAUNTING

Like Williams's narrator in Spider-Man, Blake's narrator is also haunted. What does Blake suggest about the reason for this haunting? Do you agree with him?

Discuss the setting of this story. How does the inclusion of "the voice" work in this piece?

> *Write a conversation with yourself.*

HAIR CLIPS FOR ESMA

Flavin writes, "I walked out of the hospital into the cold winter night, marveling at how the world moved on no matter what terrors happened inside." It is not unusual for individuals who are bereaved and/or traumatized to marvel with disbelief that the world continues to move as usual while theirs has stopped, so to speak. Yet during the pandemic lockdowns, for many, the world seemed to stop, leaving people feeling uncertain and unsafe. Discuss the conflicting need we have as humans for the world to stop and to continue as usual. How do you experience this as a medical professional?

Describe your reaction to the scene between Flavin's narrator and the resident who informs her of Esma's death.

Discuss the spiral notebook. How helpful do you think a reflective writing practice is, and why?

⤳ *Write about something you've shut in a drawer.*

TRAUMA BAY

Why do you suppose Arntfield delays the introduction of the pronoun "I" to the fifth stanza in this poem? Discuss what transpires between these two women. What is exposed in this poem?

⤳ *Write about what the textbook never showed.*

GRAVITY

Describe the sentence structure and pacing of "Gravity." How does it contribute to your understanding of the narrator's state of mind?

What are the reciprocal emergencies in Pittman's story?

How do Arntfield's and Pittman's pieces mirror each other?

⤳ *Write about a mirror image.*

SHELF LIFE

Discuss Stein's metaphor(s) of mortality. How does working in a high-loss environment impact your view of life and mortality?

Metaphors can cushion us from topics that are difficult to discuss head-on, such as death. Brainstorm a list of metaphors for death and discuss them.

⤳ *Write about something that expires.*

SURROUNDED

Mitchell's poem could be considered prescient in that it was written prior to the COVID-19 pandemic; however, it serves to remind us that healthcare workers' exposure to multiple deaths and deaths of "our own" are not unusual. Discuss the impact of cumulative grief. How does it show itself in your workplace? In your private life? What do you wish the general public knew that not even the pandemic has brought to light?

➤ *Write about what surrounds you.*

SECTION THREE

FALL, THEN WINTER
KACPER NIBURSKI

The following was written after spending eighteen hours in the operating room trying to save a thirteen-year-old from a motor vehicle accident.

I am thirteen and the winter is too warm and Francesco is dead. The room is a bland salmon pink, the kind that doesn't distract or lend much to decoration. Pictures pasted on the walls of rainbows and dogs and our dream future careers smell of sun and staleness. The windows are ajar. Outside shuffles with birds. Our coats weep rain. Then the teacher stands in the center of the room as she always does and we clump in our desks as we always do with our notebooks not opened, our pencils not touched, and she tells us with her hands red and nose runny and eyes not looking at us but somewhere at the walls or the salmon in them, moving, swimming, getting away from the winter without winter, that our classmate was killed in a car accident last night.

She uses the words snow squall. She says she is sorry. She says we must pray. And we do. Hands on the desks' hardwood. Eyes closed. Mouths open. Sentences tied and connected, one after another like a circle or darkness.

Our Father. Hail Mary. Apostle's Creed. Another *Our Father.* We ask to be delivered from evil while the day moves on with the birds outside and the freezing water. The teacher nods at the end. We nod too. Silence.

She then opens her hands to the ceiling that is stabbed with pencils slung from rulers and blotted with smears from food fights and tells us to describe heaven as a place. I look around the class. The heads of friends bob—Jason who has a new coat which is pretty nice and black but won't fit me and Dakota who is going to be a doctor someday and Julia with her blue painted nails and purple lipstick and eyeliner which I don't like but she does which is okay because they are her eyes and not mine. My eyes don't like eyeliner. They tried it during a ballet recital in a room with a single bar and mirrors on all three walls so you could see you seeing you, and you did, like another's eyes—better, too, because you could fix a hand and an elbow and that gut's gotta go but where except here where it is nearly lunch time and the gut growls and I haven't written anything yet. Other students are talking about the break, saying that we'll play tackle football because the mud will be mushy and full. What will be better than to be mushy and full, asks Jason. His new coat glimmers.

I think of Francesco and see his empty seat tucked in, his desk swallowing it whole. The two appear complete. I think of him and his family at my ballet recital last year with my eyeliner, my hand fixed, elbow straighter, my gut gone and good. I look to the pictures on the walls. I see Francesco's. It is of him in the NHL. And I write *heaven is hockey.*

I give it to the teacher. She reads it. She *tsks.* She tells me to take this seriously. "Your classmate just died," she says. "Kacper, please be considerate."

I go back to my desk. The walls stink of fish. The window is a screaming mouth. Rain oozes and oozes and oozes. I hear no birds. Winter has come, maybe.

CADUCEUS, TREE OF KNOWLEDGE
SHERI REDA

It's not always the serpent,
nor hunger, nor thirst,
nor yearning. Sometimes God itself
rams newly brewed poison down your throat.
Throws you out of the garden.
Calls you out
of the wings and strings you up
for no good reason. Your head hangs
vision falls
upon the place of skulls
the hollow place
and it's too late for caring
to fix anything: you should have known.

THE ANGIO
SERENA J. FOX

My father lies at the end of my white coat,
witnessing his own angiography. He jokes,
winces occasionally. The techs are reading
Malcolm X. Two vein grafts are

occluded. The internal mammary artery graft
looks good in many different projections. In
this decade, we are redirected towards the
mammary, for our hearts' blood. It

strikes me that my father has no grandchildren.
A patient of mine had his coronaries done for the
third time with a graft from his gastric artery.
Truly, the way to a man's heart...

ha ha... We have bitten of the heart and the
heart is The Tree. The serpent recoils post-op.
Not one of us is ready for the next exposure.
I did not want to

bring him here, because I did not want him to
know how easily he fits into my pocket, and
to what lengths I'll go to keep him there. My
father observed the

autopsy of his father, who walked around Miami
for a week with a massive coronary occlusion,
and he can—my fingers at his temples,
holding all I ever need

to be—watch steadily as the
dye, serpentine, drips
down the screen.

FROM BOTH SIDES NOW

ELENA SCHWOLSKY

When I left my longtime job as a nurse at the Children's Hospital AIDS Program (CHAP), my coworkers roasted me at a lively goodbye party. They presented a David Letterman-style list of the *Top 10 Reasons Why Elena is Leaving CHAP*. It started with Number 10—*She lost her beeper*. Number 4 was—*She wants to limit meetings to maximum of two hours at a time*. At Number 1, the clincher—*She wore out her funeral attire*.

In the winter of 1988, my clinic team went to a funeral every week. Families always wanted us there; we had shared intimate moments of life and death. And we showed up. In the Black Baptist churches, white-clad sisters stood in the aisles with Kleenex boxes at the ready. Haitian mourners wailed and threw themselves on the coffin. One family asked us to pose around the open casket of their berib-boned little girl. We never said no. It was the least we could do. That same winter I watched my husband struggle for breath in the night and wondered when it would be my turn to grieve.

I carried a beeper during those years, and when it buzzed against my skin it almost always meant that one of my young patients was in crisis. It meant dropping everything to respond—dinner with friends, listening to my daughter's teenage angst, relaxing in front of the TV—and rushing to the hospital. The drive was always a blur, like one of those car trips where you arrive at your destination and wonder how you got there, but the scene on the ward was full of sharp sound and focused action. Doctors and nurses crowded around a bed or a metal crib working feverishly, moving in a forest of equipment and poles, carts full of vials and syringes, until the child or baby was barely visible. My role was to comfort the family members, to explain what was happening and to keep them calm. In those moments my own feelings had to be swept into a corner of my heart, but I sometimes cried with the family when their child's last breath had merged with the air, when the poles and carts and machines were withdrawn and all that remained was a still, small child.

We were at the beginning of an epidemic whose shape and form were still mysterious and frightening—long before commercials on TV showed healthy, robust, young people taking one magical pill a day to keep the virus under control. At that time, especially for kids, a positive HIV test was equal to a death sentence, and the dying began right away in the windowless cubicle where we drew the blood and gave the results. Time stopped right then and there and divided itself into "before" and "after." I knew because I had also been on the receiving end of that terrible news.

"All you care about is AIDS," my daughter complained when I zoned out during one of her long-winded tales of high school woe. I was startled, and then defensive. I turned down invitations to the movies or dinner and only half-listened to my friends on the phone. The recitation of the events of their lives, their petty troubles, was lost in the static between stations on the radio in my head. My daughter was right, only AIDS came through clearly to me.

•　　•　　•

Letitia, the youngest daughter of Mario and Anita, stopped eating as she neared the end. I tried to get her to take a little liquid nourishment from a large syringe, and soon her bedside table was covered with syringes—chocolate, vanilla, strawberry—lined up like toy soldiers. With no energy left to talk, she would point to one, then another, and I would lift it to her chapped lips. It was a dance of sorts, choreographed by a dying girl, and when it was over her father rushed to the large window in the hallway, eleven floors above the street, and pushed against it with all his might. The window was locked, as were my feelings in that moment—locked away as I gently pried Mario's hands from the metal frame and led him to a chair in the family room.

The grief that hung over our small clinic and the families that found their way there had weight and substance, like a woolen coat wet from a sudden downpour. But there were times when we pushed it aside, hung it out to dry, and gathered as a community to share a joyous moment. The annual Christmas party was one of those times. Toys donated by local merchants piled up around our cubicles waiting to be wrapped and labeled. Dr. Jim, the rotund and jovial director of the clinic, tried on his Santa suit to be sure it still fit. And our doo-wopping singing group—AZT and the Side Effects—tuned up our unique version of "Leader of the Pack." The year that Whitney Houston made an appearance was thrilling for all of us. She was from East Orange, just up the road from the hospital, and, dressed down in a simple beige sweater and jeans, she mingled easily with the assortment of Black and Latino grandmothers, White suburban foster moms, and kids of every hue who formed our close-knit clinic family. She was unfazed by the pandemonium that ensued when Santa arrived—kids racing around the auditorium with their gifts, torn wrapping paper flying, and Whitney's voice floating above it all, singing a heartbreaking ode to the children as our future and pleading with us, their caregivers, to help them see the beauty they have inside. Our kids' lives would not be long, but we did what we could to help them feel safe, to create spaces where they could laugh.

In between special events, we moved through the ups and downs of our hectic days like a unit of medics in wartime—stopping by the ward to see kids who were in the hospital, home visits to troubleshoot treatment issues, appointments at schools and daycare centers to allay the fears of staff. We even managed, like the sarcastic docs and nurses on the TV show M*A*S*H, to find a kind of dark humor in this catastrophe. When one of our oldest patients, Keisha, age twelve, confided that she had "full grown AIDS," we chuckled together at her childish translation of that terrifying stage of her illness. And when Brenda, whose mother refused to disclose her diagnosis to her, whispered in my ear that "I think I have AIDS, but don't tell my mama because she doesn't know," we were able to appreciate together the irony in the situation that no one outside our circle could share. But the loss, the tears, the fear, and the worry could not be kept at bay for long. AIDS waited in the wings, ready to claim us again.

Some of my colleagues were able to leave their work behind when they clocked out. Home was a place for tickling their kids, playing cards on Friday night, shopping at the mall on Saturday and church on Sunday. I listened to their accounts of movies they'd seen, sleeping off a hangover, or a daughter's dance recital with a mix of envy and annoyance, aware of how different my own weekend had been. In our small, wood-paneled den I watched my husband count out his pills for the week and take his nebulizer treatment with the Sunday football game on TV in the background. Clarence made his own attempts at humor to lighten the air between us when he sighed and leaned back, frail and wan, in the beige Lazy Boy recliner that took up half the room, and I asked, "Anything wrong, honey?"

"Yeah, babe," he said, with a serious look on his face. "I think I have AIDS."

•   •   •

My friends were concerned when I accepted the job at CHAP. After Clarence's diagnosis, I had been looking for a clinic job, more or less nine to five, close to home. "But an AIDS clinic, Elena?" my friend Tami asked. "You'll be drowning in AIDS twenty-four seven." And at times I felt like I was. But Clarence had been thrust onto the frontlines of this epidemic, and the job was my way of fighting alongside him. When, after two years of a rollercoaster ride of illness and recovery, he began to lose his battle, my coworkers understood, like no one else could, and rallied around me. Boxes of groceries were magically delivered to our front door, and the lawn was mowed by unseen helpers. At work, if I needed a break to cry in the bathroom, someone stepped in to draw the blood or start the IV.

I remember begging, speaking words aloud into the musty air of the car, unwashed for months, on that last drive to the hospital. *Please, please wait, please...*I said over and over, as if there were someone listening, someone who could stop the conveyor belt that had been leading to this moment all along. Though we had slowed it down, held it back, we couldn't stop it. But *please wait,* just long enough for me to be there—to feel Clarence's warm breath on my cheek, to see him lift one eyebrow the way he did when there were no words.

His cubicle in the ICU was unnaturally quiet when I pushed aside the curtains and settled in the cold metal chair at his bedside. The beeping machines had been silenced, the blood pressure monitor and IV pole withdrawn. Only the pulse oximeter, clamped on the end of one of his long, callused fingers, sent its orange light into the room. I forced myself not to look at the monitors that told the story of Clarence's last breaths on this earth—93-90-87—they followed him down, breath by breath, into whatever lay beyond this life. After all the death-bed vigils, bearing witness to the one breath that hangs in the air and then stops in a sigh, I still had no words for this. Unlike my patients' families who drew comfort from the picture of a "house with many rooms" where their children would dwell, I had no belief in an afterlife to carry me through, no comforting picture to attach—just a sense that Clarence would continue to be a presence in my life somehow. Again, my coworkers came through, organizing a campaign throughout the clinic and hospital that provided me with enough donated vacation time to stay home for as long as I needed to.

It has been thirty years since Clarence died, almost twenty-three since I was roasted at that goodbye party. I left the clinic to go to graduate school in public health, wanting to center myself on the prevention side of the epidemic, and then spent the rest of my full-time work-life training community health workers—those underpaid and undervalued, heart-driven community educators who build a bridge between their communities and our fragmented health system. I have been retired for some years now, but every so often I'm able to engage with the work that consumed my life for a decade—teaching AIDS educators in rural Tanzania, introducing the healing power of the AIDS Quilt to people living with HIV/AIDS in Cuba and creating panels alongside them. Some of my coworkers from those early years have remained at the clinic, some have moved on, as has the epidemic. The funerals are few and far between as new treatment brings a long and healthy life to most, and effective prevention strategies have just about ended the maternal-infant transmission cycle that drove the pediatric epidemic.

Every once in a while, I take out the old photo albums—there's Brenda flashing her toothy grin, Keisha giving a thumbs up to the camera—and all the rest, dozens and dozens of beautiful children, all gone now. Healing from such accumulated loss is a long, slow process, and the stigma of AIDS which still persists despite all of the changes, complicates things. I tried a traditional bereavement group after Clarence died, joined a circle of suburban women under harsh fluorescent light in a church basement and was stunned into silence by the invitation to share my loved one's name and his cause of death. Cancer, heart failure, diabetes, cancer, a stroke, a terrible accident—so it went around the circle until it was my turn. I stumbled over the words, wondering how they would be received, steeling myself for the shock and unasked questions I would see in their eyes—how did he get it, do you have it too—and never went back. The words come more easily now. I give talks, have written a memoir, post special dates and memories on Facebook. I have a new loving partner and grandkids to watch grow.

There is one remnant of those years, one hollow place that has never filled in. "I don't cry," I tell people, to explain my dry-eyed state when all around me are weeping. I have lost both parents, a beloved sister-in-law and many friends since those years. The world has become a sad and frightening place. But I don't cry. I feel deeply, I tell myself, the tears just don't come. But sometimes, alone on a beach with the sound of the crashing waves in my ears, overcome by nameless grief, I wish they would.

AMAZING GRACE
RONDALYN VARNEY WHITNEY

I still have that one yellow rose, slipped
from my father's funeral wreath
while the guests sang. I pressed it in Corinthians 13
where it browned the text of verses 1 through 5.

Everyone sang Shall We Gather at the River and we snaked
from the parking lot to the open grave
where we thanked God for saving another soul, and ended
with Amazing Grace.

Before he died, my father drank to dull his ache. I didn't understand
chest pain or depression but I knew the words
to Amazing Grace and could harmonize
with my trained alto voice.

I sing Amazing Grace when I rock my son to sleep.
I know too much of death to sing
about boughs breaking, babies falling, no angels
coming to their call. No mother should call such a fate to a crib.

Death smells like methane—it permeates the halls
of the otherwise sanitized hospital ward. In my interview they ask me,
"What do you do when you are stressed?"
I answer, "I sing."   I never confess.

.

FINDING WHAT'S LOST
MARY C. LINDBERG

Losing leads to finding in my work. I am a chaplain at a nursing home where dozens of people die each year. Death is part of our everyday life at the nursing home, and even though it is expected, it somehow still comes as a surprise. My job includes working with residents, families, and staff, particularly at these times of grief and loss.

After someone dies, we place a flower outside that person's room. We pause to respect that person before we complete the tasks of cleaning and sending forth the body. Shortly thereafter, life at the nursing home quickly resumes its routine. There are always more people to feed and care for, more families to support. In other words, there's not a lot of time to reflect on death.

But an absence can hang in the air for weeks and months, especially with the loss of those who had been with us for a long time. Their spot feels painfully empty in the dining room, the library, the music room, or the courtyard. Jim was one of those people. Jim had been the one who sat at the corner of two hallways and always greeted passersby. Jim was also the one who played the piano in the common room every day. He wheeled up to the keyboard and escaped into his tunes, as did his hearers. Jim stood out as someone still able to communicate, joke, and reflect on his experience. He endeared himself to others by listening well and laughing often.

We all dreaded the day when Jim's cancer would claim him. He spent the last few weeks of his life in bed, rousing less and less often. I think perhaps he tried to help us get ready for his disappearance by being out of sight from his old haunts. But we would never be ready. We still miss Jim every time we walk by his room, still picture his manual typewriter sitting next to his bed. He used it to write letters to his grandchildren and pen pals.

Not every death feels as universally devastating to the staff as Jim's death did, but the losses add up. All staff members have their favorite residents, and shifting from the intimacy of daily care to the vacuum of their absence is always disorienting.

So many personalities circulate through our walls. Ohki reading her mysteries, Gary looking out the window at the dog across the street, Marlene and her jigsaw puzzles. Don't get me wrong—some deaths come as a relief. The stroke patient whose family can never get over the way that person used to be. The screamer who makes life miserable for her roommate. They leave us sometimes bereft, sometimes numb, sometimes guiltily grateful. Then we march on in a place where loss is the norm.

Families depend on us to keep going amidst life and death, to help them navigate their shifting world. They want to know, when they sit at their mother's deathbed, that others have attended such a scene before and are not as afraid as they are. Each family is different, of course. One family chattered on and on with each other as their great-grandmother neared her last breath. I wondered if they would ever get quiet and recognize the gravity of the moment. But then I realized that this was their family's style, and great-grandma might not be comfortable with them acting differently. As families reminisce, cry, laugh, sing, pray, keep silence, sip coffee, and wait, I wander in and out, trying to be sensitive to their needs. I can remember as a student chaplain being terrified of being there when someone died. Now I lean on my years of experience to help others feel less afraid. We wait, we watch, we sit in the presence of the great unknown.

Where does one put all that death? Does its accumulated weight hunch our shoulders year by year? Perhaps the losses give us perspective on our temporary status here, encouraging us not to waste quite as much time in our lives.

In the nursing home, one way we try to cope with these many losses is to invite memories to fill the empty spaces. Every month we hold a service of remembrance for those who died the month before. "We're sorry for your loss," we say as staff members and family members arrive. We gather in a candlelit room and listen as a gifted piano player offers us music and readers share words of poetry and scripture.

Everyone's favorite part of this service occurs when we read a short obituary about each person. We tell when and where that person was born, who was in their family, and what career, hobbies, and interests filled their lives. Something mysterious and uplifting happens each time we read those brief synopses, something that eclipses the sadness and heals us a bit. Our sense of losing lives is temporarily replaced with a sense of finding lives again. Inevitably, the obituaries reveal all kinds of amazing and uncanny things about the people for whom we cared, but perhaps never really knew. One woman was a nurse at the first cochlear implant. Another fellow served with General Patton. Month after month we find out colorful details about the people whom aides spoon-fed and loved; we open passages to their rich and full pasts. Deep down we always knew this to be true, but seeing a clearer picture of their lives helps us know these people we lost too.

Near the end of the service of remembrance family members break into more stories: Helga had worked as the first woman manager of a major department store and Frank used to tour with a jazz quartet. We hear not only the things they accomplished in their lives, but the habits and hallmarks that made them who they were. Stories of their pets, neighbors, quirks, humor, and core values surface. And we learn about the ways they loved. One woman's mother bought the first pair of earrings from her farmer's market booth every weekend, and when she died, she found dozens and dozens of the earrings among her mother's possessions. Our services of remembrance give us a little glimpse of life after death. We balance the losing with some finding.

OCCUPATIONAL THERAPY

VENETA MASSON

I heard it first
from the pharmacist.
The pharmacist! who delivered
her pills once a month
or whenever I phoned him.
I heard it first
first thing this morning
calling him up
for some routine thing
not news—not this news
he'd had from the sister
who'd stopped by her place
and found her
splayed out on the floor
"just cooling off"—
the sensible sister
who later thought
to phone the drugstore
to cancel all refills.

And the nurse?

Ah well, I see.
I'm not family
and not strictly business,
more like a pair
of helping hands
and a vigilant voice
at the end of the line
without a face or name.

I sit staring down
at my idled hands
and the loose ends
of another loss
unraveled in my lap.
Quick! Spool them up.
Foolish to squander sentiment
on grief, when one day you'll find
you're of a mind to take up
the threads of memory
and fabricate something practical

      a skein of remembrance
      a counterpane
      a poem

THE GOLD STARS
LARA RONAN

One by one we stand up and walk to deposit our stars. Each one is laid to rest on a bed of iridescent blue glass beads, the kind for sale at any craft store. They fill the base of a large glass bowl set upon a pretty silk scarf, signaling a special occasion. This proto-altar, invoking no particular religion or ethnicity, is temporarily set up on a Formica conference table in our academic medical center.

When our neuro-oncology team adopted this small ceremonial practice from our palliative care colleagues, I was skeptical of both the value and wisdom of creating a quarterly ritual of remembrance. After twenty-odd years of taking care of brain cancer patients, I felt that I had adapted to the patient losses, the tragic rhythm of the downward trajectory after diagnosis, and the ebb and flow of hope.

A poem opens the ceremony, something personally chosen by the leader appointed this time around. Something meaningful, somber, and hopeful. For the previous months, the section secretary has been collating the names of patients who have died. Each of us participants receives a little piece of paper, folded like a star, with the name of one lost patient that we are to read to the group. Some names prove more difficult than others to say out loud. Faces flash before our eyes. Some of the names have already dropped from our working memory and jar us like fresh bad news again. Standing up in turn to walk a star for each name over to the glass bowl makes me a little lightheaded. Time elongates as I squeeze past my colleagues around the table to reach the other side of the meeting room. The physical act of placing the star feels remarkably like shoveling the first load of dirt into an open grave. After twenty or thirty names and stars have been put to rest, a soulful gong is sounded from a hand bell to close the ceremony, and I sense the echo of a collective inward sigh as we turn to the routine tasks of the team meeting.

For a brief moment in the busyness of a day in clinical medicine, grief is invited to our table, publicly acknowledged, and then safely placed in a container to be held outside of ourselves. The observance takes our repressed, internalized sadness and releases it to the ether. That feels truly cathartic and beneficial in the moment.

The intention of the ritual is to decrease the insidious toll of unrecognized or unexpressed grief and so to avoid professional burnout and compassion fatigue in the members of the healthcare team.

I remember how embarrassed I had been during one of the earliest of these ceremonies when a few tears sneaked out. As team leader I had not wanted to show that raw emotion. My tears felt inappropriate and unearned. The names did not represent my friends or family, and I could only speculate as to what their experiences were really like. I was a mere witness to the events. Yet there was a fondness for many of these gold star patients, a sort of partnership formed in the trenches during a futile final battle that had meant something to me. Still, I viewed the loss as belonging to the families, not me, and so I felt I should not grieve. It felt presumptuous, in fact, to grieve.

Oncology had taught me to believe in the future, but over time it also taught me to believe that the future might vanish any moment. I had begun living for now while planning obsessively for a future that I would not see. This had manifested in procuring excellent life insurance coverage and teaching my children to cook, do laundry, and manage money for themselves. Unexpectedly, as I attended several of these quarterly rituals, I became aware that I had internalized these patient losses. It was only through letting some of that sadness surface and be released in the form of an origami gold star that I recognized that this sadness had become my constant companion.

It occurred to me that I had not wanted that companion. I am generally a happy person, and I know I have a happy and fortunate life. Sadness had been keeping me company while I wrote notes for the electronic medical record, while I had difficult conversations with patients about the end of life or catastrophic diagnoses. Sadness was making me leave work early to not miss a moment with my kids, but also putting me behind in my work as I sat staring out the window at the flowering trees, trying to figure out how to call back patients and families in distress. Sadness was making me ruminate, feel bad about the job I was doing, and making me irritable.

Paradoxically, the ritual that was intended to heal professional grief eventually led me to a realization that the time had come to alter my practice. When an opportunity arose to change my role in the oncology department, I knew it was time to take a break to heal, to rest and regroup. I needed to make life and joy my companions again. Instead of the rituals of collective grief, I chose to practice the rituals of family, exercise, and art-making. I immersed myself in beauty and life.

It has been a year since I stepped away from the oncology team and primary responsibilities for the care of brain tumor patients. The year away has let me heal in a way that I was not aware I needed on that day when our social worker led us though the first remembrance ceremony. Separation from the steady stream of patient loss has reinvigorated my ability to care for patients and to fully engage with their suffering. I enjoy my practice in neurology now, seeing patients with a variety of neurological conditions, including complications of cancer, but I am no longer providing treatments such as chemotherapy.

Often I think back to the day of my last ceremony with the team, when the sun shone brilliantly onto the winter snow resting on the boughs of pine trees on the hills surrounding the hospital. The morning had been cold and clear. The ceremony was no longer awkward as it had been initially, and it meant so much more to me. It felt appropriate for us to grieve collectively, even if briefly, to honor those who had been lost to us.

Acknowledgement to Linda Mason, MSW, and Sabrina Richie, RN, for championing the ceremony of remembrance for the Dartmouth-Hitchcock NCCC Neuro-oncology group.

COPY/KÄTHE KOLLWITZ

KELLEY WHITE

think hard charcoal

quick and smudged

the paper like soapstone cut

to make a woman

a child a baby

held arms folded

muscle eyes Greek

statues turned within

an embrace meant

to protect but bodies

locked Pompeii

melted Hiroshima

Dresden sinew ash

bone wreck cities

family not enough

my waiting room full

SECTION THREE
DISCUSSION AND PROMPTS

FALL, THEN WINTER

Attempting to save the life of a thirteen-year-old involved in a motor vehicle accident takes the narrator in Niburski's story back to the classroom where a teacher announces the death of a fellow student. Discuss how interactions with patients might unlock aspects of memory. Is it necessary to keep our stories out of our patients' rooms? Is it possible?

Why do you suppose Niburski tells this story through the eyes of a thirteen-year-old in the present tense, giving very particular details of setting instead of trying to articulate feelings? Which details evoke emotion most powerfully for you? How do some of those details change after the teacher regards the narrator's response as "inconsiderate?"

✎ *Write a childhood memory using the present tense.*

CADUCEUS, TREE OF KNOWLEDGE AND THE ANGIO

Why do you think Reda uses the phrase "God itself?" What does this poem suggest in terms of professional grief?

Both of these poems draw on the biblical imagery of the Tree of Knowledge and of the serpent, signaling a fall. How would you compare the difference in tone between these two poems? How does each poem treat knowledge/knowing and ignorance?

✎ *Write about knowing or not knowing.*

FROM BOTH SIDES NOW

Schwolsky's narrator states, "At that time, especially for kids, a positive HIV test was equal to a death sentence, and the dying began right away in the windowless cubicle where we drew the blood and gave the results." For many patients and families, anticipatory grief begins at the time of diagnosis. Discuss this in the context of professional grief. In what ways do professionals grieve along with patients before death occurs?

A father, a husband, a fellow classmate, co-workers, a brother. Many of the stories and poems in this book connect the deaths of patients to those personal losses that live within the professional. Some grief counselors suggest that losses are not so much healed or resolved as they are reconciled. Discuss what this means and whether you agree.

Schwolsky's story begins with an image of her supportive colleagues, and more examples of support appear in the piece. Find and discuss these.

☎ *Write about a supportive encounter.*

AMAZING GRACE

Find the reference in Whitney's poem to singing in each stanza, and compare these. What does singing have to do with the last three words in the poem?

If you were in an interview, how openly would you answer the question, "What do you do when you are stressed?"

☎ *Write about what you never confess.*

FINDING WHAT'S LOST AND THE GOLD STARS

"Everyone's favorite part of this service occurs when we read a short obituary about each person...Something mysterious and uplifting happens each time we read those brief synopses, something that eclipses the sadness and heals us a bit." ("Finding What's Lost")

"When our neuro-oncology team adopted this small ceremonial practice from our palliative care colleagues, I was skeptical of both the value and wisdom of creating a quarterly ritual of remembrance." ("The Gold Stars")

Consider Lindberg's and Ronan's statements. Discuss communal rituals of mourning. What place do they have in high-loss work environments? Of what rituals are you aware that might be appropriate for those working in high-loss environments?

The non-trivial nature of witnessing death is captured in the original Jewish tradition of *kriah*, in which anyone present at a death, relative or not, was expected to rend their garments. Do you agree that even witnessing death is of such significance that some type of expression is warranted?

☎ *Write about a healing ritual.*

OCCUPATIONAL THERAPY

What does Masson's poem suggest about the hierarchy of grief? In which other stories and poems in this book have you noticed questions about the right to grieve? A disenfranchised griever is one whose grief is not validated or sanctioned by the larger culture. Discuss how healthcare professionals might be considered disenfranchised grievers.

☎ *Write about a pair of hands.*

COPY/KÄTHE KOLLWITZ

Consider the artwork of Käthe Kollwitz. How does White use ekphrasis (a detailed description of visual art) to convey the speaker's experience of her waiting room? Find examples in the text that point to the emotions of the speaker.

Think of other examples of art that might illustrate your experience of professional grief.

✎ *Write about what is in front of you.*

SECTION FOUR

A TRIBUTE
(AND HOMAGE TO E E CUMMINGS)
PAM LENKOV

I carry your death with me,
Encumbered
I carry it in my heart

Reminder of occult frailty
The great humbler
Bane of all physicians'
Solicitude

Reconciled with family history
Of sudden loss
Now fathomable
That unseen loosening

Your valve's twin leaflets
Fatally recondite
(Deepest secret nobody knew)
Root of the malformed (aortic) root

If we'd known!
Restored by surgeon's skills
To the tree of life
Your branching path might have
Outlived
Its youthful bud

Now I/all
Who'd been perilously naive
Gather in funereal surrounds
A lamenting throng
Assailed by loss
Wondering
How the soul can hope
Listening

Your mother's tribute
Balm for the sorrowing

"An easy pregnancy
Then easy labour to bring into the world
A child with stars in his eyes, to be
Whatever a moon has meant to the earth
Whatever a sun will bring to the sky"

Oh, marvel in this encomium
Keeping your death apart
Keeping your short life
Relevant

I carry your birth with me
I carry it in my heart

NAMELESS
RACHEL FLEISHMAN

During the whispered hours of the night, the baby arrived from the delivery hospital barely alive. She was premature. Her organs were malformed. Her heart was powerless without continuous medications: one to squeeze, one to pace. Life support forced air through stagnant fluid; she was drowning. Tubes from her nose, from her mouth, from each side of her chest. Shoestring catheters threaded her belly button. Plump like a water balloon, she did not move.

Nurses connected monitors and wires, tubes and lines. Every vital sign, every lab test, every X-ray and echo more ominous than the last. Several staff raised their eyebrows, gave sideways glances. *This is not going to end well.* I knew she would die. My only goal was for this baby to meet her mother; intensive care merely pausing death. My team moved on with hourly blood tests, each drop of blood prompting constant manipulations of medications and ventilation.

These things are not gentle.

We almost lost her more than once. Her breathing tube would fill with the same yellow fluid draining through tubes jammed between her ribs. No breath; ventilator alarm. No heartbeat; monitor screaming. Our team of doctors and nurses ran to her bedside, each time poised to compress her chest, knowing that if we started, she would not survive, would never meet her mother. With rapid force, I threaded a thin plastic catheter down her breathing tube and slid it back out. With this suction came thick secretions. And with their removal, she would regain her life as quickly as she'd lost it. After each spell, I let out a sigh to re-center myself, to remind myself she had to wait for her mother.

We staved off death for two days before her mother arrived from the birth hospital. Two days of lability, two days replacing her body fluids with manufactured nutrition and someone else's blood. Two days when I paced and hovered, not sure if her baby could make it. Her mother arrived with a gnarled sweater over her hospital gown. A man in tight jeans and a black leather coat escorted her, two steps ahead, never by her side, teardrops tattooed below his eye. He barely spoke her language.

The unit secretary handed her a form to sign. She held the pen with an unpracticed grip, wrote an X. My gut clenched. To avoid embarrassing her further, we asked the man to write down her information while she arched back into a tall green chair meant for nursing mothers. He wrote a name that was different from the name on this mother's delivery records, scribbled an address that Google could not find.

Be a doctor, one of my mentors used to say. *You have the power of influence, the power of narrative.* The junior doctor, a native Spanish speaker, helped me steer. We did not sit by the baby while we spoke because we could not fit our bodies beside the equipment sustaining her life. We presented very little of the raw data of her demise to her mother. We skipped the unending jargon, each term likely a symptom of absent prenatal care aligned with bad luck.

Instead, we spoke plainly. *She's too early, her heart did not form properly and does not beat well, she cannot breathe.* We apologized. *We cannot save your daughter. Ella va a morir.* The mother clenched her hand to forehead. Silent. No tears. Barely breathing.

I moved to squat beside her, put my hand on her hand. I crouched so long that my legs cramped, but I held steady beside her. The room filled with sadness. The man took a step backward, leaning against the wall. He was silent, pulled the brim of his hat down over his face. And in this silence, I felt a release because we had made it to this moment of truth telling.

"How can we help you remember your daughter?" I asked.

She seemed so scared. Scared of her daughter dying, of the man with her, of our team who did not know her. "No quiero Bautismo. No quiero fotografias," she said. She would not hold her child. I wondered what forces—internal or external—might prevent a mother from wanting these things.

We took a few photos, just of the baby's face, and slid them into a memory box in case she changed her mind. No phone calls. No family. Nurses molded teensie footprints into clay. Heart-shaped pendants lay across the baby's swollen, jiggling chest.

"Capturing her heartbeats," I explained.

I wanted to find a way to connect with her, but felt only the anguish of powerlessness. The woman would not make eye contact with us. She looked to the man for a nod before she answered our questions. The social worker, the junior doctor, and I noted her fingers clenching and unclenching the arm of the chair. We took stock of the barcode tattooed on her chest, the bruising inside her wrists, the gaze fixed on the floor.

We orchestrated time alone with her before her daughter died to ask if she was being trafficked for sex, if she was safe. She flinched. Said she was fine. We offered her the safety of the hospital and she only looked at her feet, big toes peeking through worn leather. The junior doctor spoke to her alone in Spanish. But the man came back in quickly and never left her side again.

I walked her to the bedside and encouraged her to look at and touch her child. The padded tip of her first two fingers nuzzled into the arch of a foot, thumb stroked toes the way dew slides down a blade of grass in the early morning. Then she left, one step behind the saunter of a leather jacket, curtains of hair shadowing her face from the light.

A nurse held her baby. We turned off the medicines sustaining her heartbeat. The practiced hands of a respiratory therapist squeezed breath after breath into her body. I peeled thick white strips of tape from her upper lip, trying not to tear her premature skin. I slid the tube from between her lips and we waited, calm. Quickly, her heart stopped beating. She died. Gently.

Later, I sat huddled over the speakerphone in my office with the same junior doctor. I had been crying. We had practiced the words. *Tu hija murió. Lo siento mucho.* We never heard the mother's voice again; her phone had run out of minutes. One of us tried to reach her every day for weeks. Nothing.

This woman, this mother, haunts me. I wonder, often, if I could have helped her if I had had more time. The baby gave us all the time she had. And in this brief window of her life, I pushed for a compassionate death for her child, to avert excessive needles and transfusions and brute force CPR, to be a doctor. But without time, we did not have the quiet moments of trust. Trust built hour by hour at her child's bedside. Trust to see me, see our team, as allies. Trust to believe we could help her. I can still feel her when I enter that room in our NICU. I could control the moment and tenor of her daughter's death, could enable an intimate touch between mother and child. But I could not help her. When this mother left us to recover from her cesarean, from the few moments she'd spent with her child, she left the hospital with a man who did not know her name. Or the name of her dead daughter.

PASSING THROUGH
JOSEPH BOCCHICCHIO

Had I not gone on vacation Nathaniel Deacon might still be alive. The last time I saw him was Christmas Eve. He was sickly and thin, but no more than usual. He had been in and out of the hospital in recent weeks with no real improvement in his condition. This, too, was normal. Nathaniel never got better. The best we could ever expect was for him to be stable. I went to his apartment to check on him and found him propped up on his futon. He was without a shirt, and his arms were outstretched on either side draped over pillows. He was weak. "I'm tired, man," he said. We fist bumped as I put out ten bottles of sugarless sports drink for him. "You owe me ten bucks for this," I told him. "When I get my check, I'll square up with you," he replied. He was always good for the money I fronted him. Not this time. He would be dead by New Year's Day.

I knew Nathaniel for more than ten years as he drifted in and out of my caseload. He was a bright young guy, poorly educated but with a native intelligence and a curiosity that ranged from the profound to the ridiculous. He quoted Milton, and he would talk with equal fervor about quantum physics and the abominable snowman. He was thirty-two when he died, so I had thirty years on him. He seemed childlike to me and he was, in fact, childlike. Nathaniel was not, however, an innocent. He was a con man and a thief, a doper and a dealer, careless with women and with fire. He left a trail of children behind him and at least one burned down house. He grew up troubled and ill and never got things right. Nathaniel Deacon was a catastrophe.

He was barely twenty when he first showed up on my caseload. He was healthier then and at his fighting weight of about 175 pounds. A natural street fighter, he was also fresh from training for four years straight as a boxer. His movements betrayed him; he was all smooth and alert like a liquid animal, quick to assess people and situations, looking for opportunities and weaknesses while at the same time schmoozing it up to get on your good side. Nathaniel was dangerous.

He came from a dangerous family. His father was a local hood who ran dope and women. He came to me after Nathaniel was first assigned to my caseload. He was lean, muscular and tawny like a lion. "You Joe?" he asked.

"Who's asking?" I replied.

"I'm Deacon, Nate's dad." I nodded yes. He put his hand out and we clasped arms old-school style, like blood brothers.

"You take good care of my boy now," he said. His voice hovered between a plea and a threat. I took it as both, looked him in the eye, and told him I would. I never saw him again. The last time Nathaniel saw him was some five years later. They came to blows, and Nathaniel wasted him. Nathaniel was out of the county at the time and off my caseload, but when he told me about it years later I believed him. We often talked shit, trading stories about fights we had; he from the ring and the streets, me from the streets and martial arts. He showed me his cross-saw punch which I told him was a lot like a move in the Sun style. I can't throw a cross-saw without thinking of him.

When he was a little boy, Nathaniel was playing on a third-story porch. It was cluttered with bric-a-brac and debris, broken furniture, and skids. He must have been three at the time, as he tells it. He told me the story often, and it didn't change much in the telling. How he was out there alone, his parents drinking and doping it up inside the house. He wasn't being watched; Nathaniel was never being watched. He got up on top of the junk and fell over the railing. There began his fall; pitched over backwards looking up, wind rushing up around him, arms outstretched, not enough time to cry out, the sudden impact and a young life ruined. It took him seconds to fall and decades to die.

Nathaniel sustained a traumatic brain injury. His skull was fractured just above the pre-frontal lobe, damaging the neo-cortex. A four-inch scar was evident just at the hairline which at the time of his death was just beginning to recede. His pancreas was also wrecked, leading to his lifelong dependency on insulin. In addition to diabetes he had developed gastroparesis, hypertension, arteriosclerosis, neuropathy, and macular degeneration after a lifetime of abuse and neglect. Along the way he had his gallbladder removed, had broken a number of bones, suffered some nasty lacerations, and had a mouth full of bad teeth. When he died, Nathaniel was legally blind, five-foot-nine and a 107 pounds. Cause of death was probable stroke. They didn't do an autopsy after he died. There was a lot they didn't do while he lived.

Nathaniel Deacon was a pain in the ass. He lied all the time. His didn't show up for appointments. He didn't take his meds unless he could get high on them. Over the years in which he came and went from my care, I did what I could to get him stable. He was homeless on and off, usually between girlfriends. In my line of work that is not unusual. Nathaniel would disappear when he got an offer to crash somewhere. He would seek me out when all else failed.

. . .

The last time he came to me, he had bottomed out. A social worker from Pennsylvania called; Nathaniel had been admitted to a local hospital and was raising hell. He was homeless and threatening suicide if they discharged him. His last address was in my county. Nathaniel had given them my name and agency, so he was referred back to me.

I worked with the staff at the hospital to transition him back to his home county. The plan was to put him on a bus back here and for him to stay in a shelter until I could link him up with services. Nathaniel was not good with plans and got off the bus before the state line. After numerous phone calls with social workers, cops, and bureaucrats, Nathaniel Deacon was put in the back seat of a patrol car and hustled back to town, where he holed up in a cheap motel, homeless, out of food, and without medicine.

I knew this motel. It was a low-down, run-down, down-and-out joint, a sinkhole for bottom feeders, a place where you went when you had no choice or didn't want to be found. Each room had one small window and a door that opened onto a narrow unpaved parking lot that was littered with trash and scored with potholes.

The last time I had been at this place I had been tracking down someone with a severe psychotic disorder. His name was Marty. He was reported to have booked a room there. When I'd arrived, he was outside his room, crazy as a shit house rat. I knew him well. Marty was usually very organized and lucid. Not this time. Pure word salad and whistling was all he was capable of. I couldn't engage him at all. He retreated back into his room, so I called into the office for direction. We decided to call the police. They arrived and knocked on Marty's door. He refused to open and the manager, not surprisingly, was not around to provide a pass key. The cops tested the door, found it flimsy, and proceeded to kick it in. As it gave way Marty came crashing out, swinging a razor knife. This was not good. The officers called for backup as they pulled their Tasers out. One lead sunk in after another, but Marty kept coming at the cops. More cops arrived, more leads bit into Marty. He soon had enough leads into him to make him look like a marionette, but the Tasers didn't faze him. Marty kept swinging the razor, culling an officer from the pack and getting close enough to cut. I was certain they would shoot him and wanted to turn away. But I kept looking, figuring I'd have to report the outcome anyway, when suddenly they tackled him. Marty was covered by blue uniforms, and when he emerged he was cuffed but still struggling. An ambulance arrived, and he was put on the gurney in four-point restraints and taken to the emergency room. Later I found out his thyroid had crashed, causing the psychosis and violence. The ER doc said he would have died had he not gotten treatment.

All this flashed before me as I knocked on Nathaniel's door at the motel. "Who is it?" he yelled. The voice was familiar but different.

"Joe," I answered, standing off to the side of the door out of habit. You never know what's on the other side.

"Come in," he answered. I slowly pushed the door open, paused, and walked in. Nathaniel was lying on the bed fully clothed watching an old Kung Fu movie.

"I love this movie," he said, as if it hadn't been almost six years since he last saw me.

"Yeah, me too," I said, playing into the part. "So what's up?" I asked. Nathaniel was silent. I scoped the room. It was just big enough for a bed, nightstand, microwave, dorm-size fridge and TV. The bathroom had no shower, just a sink and toilet. The toilet had blood in it but no stools.

"You been throwing up again, Nathaniel?" I asked.

"Yeah, real bad. Can't keep nothing down no more. I'm starving, I got no food, no money and I can't stay here no more."

"You got any meds?" I asked, knowing the answer.

"No, man. And I'm sick."

I took him to the ER and braced myself for the ordeal to come. Not mine, but Nate's.

       •   •   •

Here's the thing about going to the emergency room. It helps for you to have an emergency. The staff gets cranky when people with chronic illnesses come in, especially if they are "frequent fliers," have a history of not taking care of themselves, are manipulative, and are prone to throw their urine sample at you. Especially if you are Nathaniel Deacon.

"What brings you in today, Nathaniel?" the triage nurse asks. She keeps her distance and looks at me. I look at Nathaniel.

"I'm sick. I just don't feel good." The nurse looks at me. I look at Nathaniel.

"My stomach hurts, I can't keep nothing down, I'm starving, no one is listening to me, and no one is helping. I'm dying." The nurse looks at me.

I tell her his medical history. She says, "Yes, we know Nathaniel very well."

They don't know shit about Nathaniel, I think to myself. They know him as a cluster of signs and symptoms and an array of bad behaviors. They don't know he has siblings he has never met, that he spent three weeks in the burn unit when he was four years old, that he had a bit part in a movie, that he is a Buckeye fan, that he likes turtles and birds, and that his grandmother calls him a nigger. They don't know that he has been falling for thirty years.

118

She walks out of the pod and we wait. We wait a long time. Nathaniel is a GOMER, which translates as Get Out of My Emergency Room. Nate and I bullshit and watch TV, and in between I coach him: "Be cool with the staff. They want to help; let them do their job."

The nurse comes back with a partner and then the pain starts. They have to draw blood. Nathaniel's veins are shot from the diabetes, a fact I have mentioned. They get started looking for a vein anyway. They run their fingers down his arms, start tapping his skin. They set a tourniquet, slapping and tracing his veins again. They move down to his hands, they think they have something, they stick him and nothing, they move elsewhere, again nothing, they stick him again, and again, and again. Nothing. I tell them he usually ends up needing a PIC line. They ignore me.

Nathaniel is prone, half sitting up, like Marat in his bathtub. "They're torturing me, man," he says. I put a hand on his shoulder and nod. The record for sticking Nathaniel is twenty-six times, including his groin, with no draw. We aren't close to breaking a record yet, but Nathaniel is getting testy. "Fuck this," he says. "I wanna go home." He forgets he is homeless.

"Not yet," I tell him. The nurses scatter and pull the curtain behind them. Soon I see the tactical boots and blue pants below it. Cops, of course. They stay outside the room for now. A male technician comes in wheeling a sonogram machine. He plasters Nate's arm with gel and applies a probe, rolling down the veins while the eerie interior of his arm comes into view on the monitor. "I'm thirsty," says Nate, "I need something to drink, and my sugar is dropping."

"Not yet," says the tech. "We need to get blood first." He keeps rolling the probe. He thinks he has a vein and goes for it but hits a nerve. I had placed myself at Nate's free arm to block a punch should he throw one. Nate stiffens and yells but keeps his hands to himself. The cops peek in.

"What the fuck!" yells Nathaniel. "What are they here for?" I quietly ask Nathaniel to be cool. "Shit, he says, shaking his head, "I just wanna go home."

Here's the thing about somebody like Nathaniel. He broke his fucking head and damaged the part of his brain that the rest of us use when we are in a tight spot. The part that helps us plan and make good decisions, keep a cool head, tolerate and cope with adversity. The part that prevents us from going off and punching someone right in the face. The other thing about somebody like Nate is that he is moody because of his erratic blood sugar levels. Throw in chronic pain and blindness and you have the makings of a real jumpy guy. So when I bring him to the ER, I tell them all about his medical history, all the resultant difficulties Nathaniel faces and presents. I explain about his lifeless veins, how he usually needs a PIC line. They tell me that their protocols don't allow for a PIC line and continue to stick him. I think to myself *fuck you and your protocols.* About four hours into this effort, they finally find a vein, get some blood, start an IV, give him something for his nausea and pain, feed him and get him admitted. The following evening he leaves against medical advice, just like I knew he would. He disappears again into the half world of sickness and crime. Nathaniel had just been passing through. He was always just passing through.

.   .   .

The winter came on hard and turned Siberian. Daytime temperatures stayed in the single digits and dropped below zero at night. Winds were high and snow took on an otherworldly aspect in the form of small tunnel shaped clusters that rolled across the frozen landscape. People were being found frozen to death. One person who lived on the streets crawled into a metal donation bin and burrowed into the clothing there in an effort to stay alive. It didn't work. Another man had died crammed into a tight space under a bridge. An old woman locked herself out of her house and froze to death on her front porch. I developed frostbite in my fingers while trying to convince a homeless psychotic man, who was oblivious to the cold, to take shelter. I kept busy with my caseload and didn't have time or resources to think about Nathaniel. He was just one of many and would turn up at some point when he needed help, or maybe he would die somewhere.

He showed up when he ran out of money. I got him hospitalized and he agreed to go to the shelter when stable. I took him down to the city shelter and this time he hung tight to the plan. "Nathaniel," I told him. "Stay put or take your chances on the street. I can't fix this if you don't listen. If you don't listen, the chances are you won't live."

"I know," he answered, "I know."

He looked like shit. He'd lost about thirty pounds since the time I had first met him. He needed a cane to walk due to neuropathy and the ulcers on his feet. His post-hospital orders were a treatment plan buffet, so I got him hooked up with a primary care physician and a cadre of specialists: an endocrinologist, a nephrologist, a podiatrist, a gastroenterologist, psychiatry and counseling.

Being in the shelter was hard for him. It's hard for all the homeless. They spend their days outside unless the weather is too cold to survive. Inside it is crowded and uncomfortable. Fights break out. Serious fights, with broken legs in bathroom brawls. At night they sleep on single cots in a vast room the stench of which lives in your nostrils long after you get outside.

After about a month of his being in the shelter, I secured stable housing for Nate. Despite constant support and direction, Nathaniel couldn't learn how to take care of himself. He never took his blood sugar levels, ate poorly, didn't take his insulin correctly, stopped his psych meds, and forgot to take his blood pressure medication. He threw up most of what he ate. All the doctors would tell him what to do, how and why, but Nathaniel seemed to be unable to learn. "It's like I'm in denial," he would say. "I need to be put someplace where I can be taught how to take care of myself. I'm dying, man. I'm dying."

Nathaniel continued to decline despite frequent trips to the emergency department, hospital admissions, and outpatient appointments. I found him a visiting nurse and services for the blind. I worked with his medical case manager to get him into a skilled nursing facility for short-term medical rehabilitation. We were told he didn't meet criteria. This, I thought, is how the poor die now. They die from protocols, efficiencies, best practices, and criteria inherent in the machinery and money of medicine.

When I told him he couldn't get into rehab, he wept. "Fuck this, man. I give up," he said.

I told him he was down but not out, that he had to take the standing eight count, get back to his corner, towel down and hydrate, and get back in for the fight. I told him, "I don't back losers or quitters." He put his hands out in small fists as if he had his gloves on. I tapped them with mine, but I knew he was finished.

•   •   •

A little more than a year had passed since I had Nate on my caseload. He had made some progress. He had stable housing and furniture. His money was being managed for him. He had cable TV and a phone. He had a parrot and a parakeet. He had a turtle but couldn't bear to see it always trying to get out of its tank, so he had set him free before the autumn came. Nate was thin and frail like a holocaust victim, always thirsty and hungry. The toilet bowl always had blood in it. He was back in touch with his mother who came to see him often. She was a troubled woman with health problems of her own, but there was real affection between them. She knew she hadn't raised him right, but then maybe nobody could have.

I had scheduled Nate to see the nephrologist. Nate cancelled because he didn't want to find out about something else he couldn't fix. The doctors withdrew his pain meds and his anxiety medication, saying it was bad for his gastroparesis. I didn't think it made much difference, given how sick he already was. When I stopped by to see him before my vacation I told him he needed to fight this, take control of his health, eat right, monitor his blood sugar levels, take his insulin and other meds. I told him I would fight just as hard as he would. He smiled weakly and said, "Thanks for taking such good care of me."

As soon as I was away, I worried. I had my colleagues back at the office call him once a day. About three days after Christmas, while still on the road, I got one last voice mail from Nathaniel: "Hey man, it's me, Nate. Hey, you got your people tracking me down, but I'm okay. I mean I'm just me, sick and everything, but I'm okay. I'm gonna spend some time with my family, my nieces and nephews and just chill, you know? It's Christmas. You have a good holiday. I love you, man, and thanks for everything."

I cancelled the follow up calls and spent the week with my family, my far-flung children and grandchildren. My wife Vicki and I counted our blessings and numbered them among the stars. On the way back from dropping off my granddaughter in Pennsylvania I picked up a voice mail from Nate's mom. Nate hadn't returned her calls. She had become worried, went to him, and found him dead. Her voice cracked in the telling.

When I called her back, I listened to her cry gently as she told me how she'd found him. He had died alone, having collapsed between the kitchen and living room, dried blood on his face. She said that Christmas with Nate and the family had been good, and she was happy they had their time together. I told her I was glad for them and sorry for her loss, and that it was a loss for me as well. We hung up, and it ended there.

I saw his long tumble downward: his freefall, silent but for the rush of his pulse fading in his head, legs giving way, Nathaniel pitching forward towards the ground, dying eyes failing. His fall goes unbroken: the crash and then the stillness, the absolute stillness as he comes to rest at last.

Vicki placed her hand on mine and I cried quietly for a while as we drove down the winter hills of Pennsylvania. Flat Ohio and home were on the horizon. I put the seat back and stretched out. Nate, I recalled, was just passing through.

YOU LEAVE THE ROOM
WILLIAM A. FRENCH

You leave the room with
blood on your hands, with
a dead man's blood
drying to a burgundy glaze
on your helpless hands.

You leave the room while
adrenaline's sweet sting
still tingles your cortex, while
the discord of chaos
still echoes heavy—
a lead church bell
through the silence of death.

You leave the room with
blood on your hands, but
feel only the urgent thrust
of your own blood
as it surges along the endless
circuit, sustaining life by looping
through an uncaring heart.

A BIT IN THE TEETH

JAFAR AL-MONDHIRY

The room was hot. Not a sweltering, humid kind of heat, but an unbearable stuff-iness that weighed on me, heavier and heavier, in that dilated moment of anxiety. We were stuck there in Frank's room with his wife, his sisters, his medical team, palliative care doctors, residents, fellows, attendings, and finally me—the last to arrive. There are not a lot of good places in the hospital for a crowd this size to meet for an intimate conversation, so his bed was the hearth around which we gathered. It had been the right decision to come, but the sweat in my body made a decision to try and leave.

Beyond the shirt and tie, the white coat, and the likely unnecessary contact gowns for his past MRSA exposures, there were many layers of separation between us. I tried peeling them away with some easy questions first. How's the pain? Can you still sleep? Get to the bathroom? How's the physical therapy coming along? Who are these lovely ladies with you today?

His grin was incredible. For all the breakdown happening around him and inside of him, he had these big, fiercely white teeth, and he helped us all by not keeping his smile to himself. His hope was infectious, and I wanted what he had for others. Just not for him, not right now.

And so that smile became a wall, high and forbidding, holding out against my words. Was I wrong? People outlive statistics all the time. Still, no matter what happened with his prostate cancer, the damage to his spinal cord was done. Eviscerate every bad-acting cell in his body, and he still would never walk again. But the war raged on, his war against his cells, and I was being conscripted to the losing army.

"I can beat this, Doc. You never seen anyone like me," he said.

He was right about that much, but maybe that said more about me and my recent entry into the field. Here he was, decimated by a cancer of the elderly at forty-one years old. Bedbound, twenty pounds gone in the last three months, multiple pulmonary emboli, recurrent pleural effusions, painful and debilitating spinal metastases, all piling up on him with time. In spite of all this, his eyes were crystal clear, taking me all in from the moment I stepped through the threshold of his room, sizing me up in every dimension. They made me second guess my every word, each one being either the counseling of a professional or the stumbling of a novice. I felt a dull ache forming near the center of my back from trying to hold a rock-steady, upright posture, leaning in from the edge of the vinyl-pleated hospital chair across from the large circle formed around his bed. If I didn't know my lines, I at least had to look the part. I had to find the confidence to destroy his.

"I'm really worried about what's happening with your cancer," I said.

I knew I was committing myself to a long talk, so I purposefully had asked for this to be the last stop of the day. And it had been quite a day, rounding on all the inpatients that morning, taking in many calls for help on new consults, then clinic through the afternoon, all of which made me late to this gathering. It felt like a long journey just getting to his room that day, but we still had a rough road to travel from where he thought he was to where we actually were. We had to find each other using two different maps, so I asked him to describe what he saw around him.

"Look," he said firmly. "I wake up each day with the faith that I have the strength to do the next right thing. That's all I can do."

Dodging the question—a covert and maybe effective form of denial. He seemed too strong-willed, too emboldened to be as sick as he was. Despite his optimism, his reality was too harsh to avoid confession, and the truth was that life had been tough these past few months. A previously robust, competitive triathlete, getting out of bed was now a herculean effort, and happened no more than once or twice a day. It's always hard for people to lose the basic dignity of normal bathrooming, but I didn't hear an ounce of self-pity in his voice. The strained look on the faces of his family spoke of different emotions.

"I do every exercise the physical therapist can give me, two times a day," he said, his volume climbing with his determination. "I'm up at 6 a.m. and out in the hallways before anyone else."

Finding control within the uncontrollable. I could see right through it, but I still admired the hell out of him for his spirit. He had this unshakable commitment to himself that abided all tragedy.

As usually happens in these talks, impatience gets the better of people, and the question of treatments was pressed on me early. After a few attempts at deflection to get him to tell me more about symptoms, what he liked and didn't like about the life forced on him by his cancer, this painful world that his doctors could not protect him from, I, too, was cornered into a confession: "I don't think the medicines are helping the cancer anymore, and I worry that anything else we try is just going to make things worse."

His eyelids drooped down with some recognition of the ugliness I was offering, but he kept his smile bright and out front, in between us. "So, what's next then?"

The expectant looks of all the other people in the room started to stack up on me. I felt the blood rush to my face in a hot flush under their stares. My heart rate climbed, and my mouth went dry. *Take a pause. Give it space. You can't solve this for them.* I took the bit in my teeth and kept us walking down the inevitable path. "We've tried a lot of therapies for this, and I'm sorry it hasn't—"

"Don't be sorry," he interrupted. "Who's sorry? That's the way it is, but I need to see where we go from here."

"Even in the best-case scenario, your walking, your activity—we can't make those better," I said helplessly. *Can it get much worse? How does he live like this?* "And everything has been happening at such a rapid pace, we won't be able to meaningfully change the fact this cancer is going to take your life."

"You don't *know* that. You *think* that, but you're just a man, and only God knows what will happen to us," he said, shifting in the bed, pushing his elbows into the mattress to lean himself forward, his face strained and huffing with the smallest physical effort. "It's our job not to give up on life."

"I'm not giving up on you; no one is giving up on you," I said, jumping to reassure him. *How the hell do I argue with Divine Providence?* "We just don't want to do things that will make your situation worse. You're right, I'm not God, but it's important to talk about what we usually see in these cases, what's most likely to happen. I just don't want you to miss an opportunity to see someone or do something important with what time you have left." At this point the family started to squirm, their faces turning away. I had dealt an intentional blow, inviting his mortality into the room, but he was still blocking the door.

"We're doing something important right now—we're saving my life," he said. "You seem like a good guy, but I don't know if you're up for the job."

He was dead right. I wasn't up for the job, and I was only just recently employed in it. A fellow in my first year, I was only partially involved in his journey to this point. After seeing him in the clinic twice, I was now the inpatient consult fellow left with the difficult job of summarizing his long list of experiences with other, much more skilled doctors. All the evidence in the world wouldn't let me speak in their place, at least not right now. I could see where he was on his map, and we would get no further. He took a glimpse at mine and pushed it back to me. Not today.

"You're wrong, but I still love you," he said.

Another long pause.

"Okay," I said. Everything in me wanted to say more. I had to get him just a little further, or at least make him feel better after what I tried to inflict on him, but the best thing I could do at that moment was…nothing. I didn't force a discussion about his code status, what we should do next, his home care situation, hospice referral. I just thanked him for talking with me, and he thanked me back.

"Would it be okay if I came back tomorrow?" I asked.

"We got something else to talk about?" The smile was gone now, reserved for better people maybe. He said it with a snappy oh-so-now-you've-changed-your-mind? tone. I was either on his bus or off it. But here I was, still begging for him to pull over.

"I just want to see how you're doing," I said. "I know sometimes questions come up after we leave these meetings." *Leave this door open, please—there's so much pain waiting for you down the road you're going.*

"Yeah, okay. Fine," he grumbled.

This time I smiled. The best he could give me back was half a smile, no teeth, lips curled back in restraint, eyes drifting out to another corner of the room. I shook his hand and left. *Please don't hate me. There's love in all this, I swear.*

The next day I came, and we kept it superficial. I asked if he thought about any of the things we spoke about the day before, and he said he'd think it over and talk about it when he got out of the hospital. I breathed a huge and admittedly selfish sigh of relief, not wanting to upset this man any more, and not being pinned down into fixing his cancer right now, the way so many others in his shoes have demanded of me in similar situations on the consult service. Sure, I still had a lingering disappointment about not being able to convince him about the virtues of hospice, but that, too, had a kind of selfishness in it. Here I was, feeling diminished just because I didn't change his entire worldview in one conversation.

And so I left again, this time crossing his name off my list like so many other consults for family meetings that came and went with no conclusion. His memory came back to me a month later, but at that point I couldn't even bring to mind enough details to find his chart in the electronic medical record. In broad strokes I already knew his fate, but a morbid curiosity drew me back: Would he make it back to clinic? When would that next talk happen?

Every few months I would try and look back at the patients I collided with in the hospital while on the inpatient services across all of our different sites. Without fail, at least half were dead. For those whose status was unclear, who had been so sick that their need for care had been frequently registered in the chart, a steep drop-off in notes suggested they were now also gone—a digital departure prefiguring their physical death.

And so I've come to expect these disappearances, not only "out of sight, out of mind" but truly gone from this world. Far too many to count, let alone remember with any depth. Even when a patient and I did share moments of powerful significance—as I had with Frank—the black parade of new cases drowned out the feeling. Still, at times I could read back through my own notes and recapture some of that emotion, that presence with the patient, hidden somewhere within the sterile language of prognostication and the calculus of treatment risks. Often, that's all I had left of the experience, these little scraps of formal writing that so crudely outline the medical journey of the soul from the body.

But I couldn't find his chart, and so I was left to wonder what others had written about Frank and what that might tell me about his fate, about his defiant hope. Of course he would leave us, but at what point would that smile leave him? Had I taken it away that day I read his prophecy? I had not been wrong, and eventually Frank would have understood that. Would he still love me anyway?

A BEAUTIFUL MESS
TEEGAN MANNION

The heavy dressing room door swings shut behind me, and as soon as I hear the comforting click, I put my pet bucket and lunchbox barn on the floor, pull my red nose off so it hangs by its elastic around my neck, move a rogue bottle of Virox out of the way to set my big straw hat on the wooden wheelbarrow, and drop forward over myself. Elbows on knees, head toward the ground, I feel the blood return to my brain and the compression in my back start to ease. I rub the crease left across my cheeks from the taut, white elastic that has held my nose in place all day. It stings.

The lights in our long, narrow, storage-closet-turned-dressing-room are on, which means Jamie, my clown partner, is around and I'll probably be seeing him soon. The bare bulbs over the three mirrors and three dressing tables glow like Broadway, reminding me of all those sweet years of performing in musicals long before I became a professional therapeutic clown. Full of passion, purpose, and optimism, I had no room in myself for death or any other endings back then, and I hadn't yet learned that the tender place behind my sternum might require more than bone for protection.

At the far end of the room is a window, and outside on the ledge is a nest of baby pigeons. We've been watching them get ready to fly. Over the window is a set of dusty, old, white blinds with a rainbow stripe running down the middle. Even though the office across from ours in the adjacent wing of the hospital is usually dark, we keep the blinds shut most of the time, not only to keep our nakedness to ourselves while changing, but as importantly, to cloak the secret transformation from civilian to clown and back, protecting the mystery and the magic—no one wants to look out their window and see a half-human clown eating a sub. For some reason they're open right now.

I walk to my purple chair and sit down. I watch the door, and while I wait for it to open, I tug at my hangnail and think about Tina.

•   •   •

It's Tina's birthday. She's finally five. The thing she's been most excited about is starting kindergarten. She's been looking forward to the teacher on staff here at SickKids coming to her room with worksheets to practice numbers and letters, shapes and colors. Tina has told me over and over how wonderful it will be to be a big kid, to learn and to be rewarded with stickers for her work. Every time she's told me, her whole face has come to life like there were light bulbs screwing into place behind her eyes, and a small wiggle like a shiver would start in her middle and spread throughout her body until she popped out of bed like toast from the toaster. So today is the big day: Tina is officially a big kid.

Tina is one of my closest long-term patient-friends, and I see her every day that I work. For most of our year-and-a-half relationship she's been in isolation, which means that our play always began with a door between us. I'd pause in the hall, knock gently, and after catching her eye, I'd begin the difficult process of donning my personal protective equipment, which, despite being a daily procedure, I could never seem to get quite right.

I would take a faded yellow gown from the top of the clean, folded stack and shake it out like a parachute, letting it fall through the air and over my head and shoulders, landing like a wash of golden yellow Rapunzel hair, complete with two neat ribbons to tie under my chin. The yellow fabric of the gown over top of the wide brim of my costume's straw hat made me look more like a beekeeper than a princess, but I modeled my new look proudly, making kissy photo-shoot faces through the window to Tina's delight.

Between bursts of raucous laughter, she'd shout "No, Rose, not like that!" and shake her head. Oh right, I remember now. I'd remove my golden hair and stretch one long leg into the sleeve of the yellow gown, pulling it up the length of my leg while pointing my toes toward the sky in my best standing split. Not a very graceful dancer, there was much hopping and toppling. Tina would climb up and stand on her bed, so our faces were at the same height, and shake her head and bounce up and down. "No, Rose, no no no!"

I'd continue by pulling two blue latex gloves over my pink ballet flats, giving myself extra-long floppy toes, and then hook a blue paper mask over each ear so they dangled by their elastics like long earrings. Tina guffawed. Despite how many times she'd seen me do this, watching me get it wrong never seemed to get old. She waited by her door every afternoon for me to enact this goofy business.

Finally, with Tina's guidance and permission, I would manage to suit up properly and enter her room looking almost like anyone else: full gown covering my

'Rose' clothes, gloves on hands, mask obscuring all but my eyes, red nose smooshed underneath. Only my over-sized glasses and straw hat piled high with fake fruit and silk flowers identified me as someone who was not going to reposition her IV or change her ostomy bag.

We moved through a predictable order of activities each visit, which came to be a comfortable way to shape our time together. There was a safety in the structure and a sense of ritual in the routine. I made sure a visit from Rose was consistent and reliable for Tina in a place where not much else was.

First, we'd blow bubbles. On the occasion when contact precautions weren't in place and I didn't have to wear a mask, I'd blow and she'd pop. Sometimes she did both the blowing and the popping, and I'd hold the magic bubble bear, whose wand rose from his top hat when magical kid fingers were waved over the opening, and try to catch bubbles on my nose. We built forts out of the sofa cushions which became her convenience store where I bought very expensive bananas from her. Bananas reminded us of Boots, the monkey on Dora the Explorer, and we'd remember that it was almost time for our favorite show. Her mom or dad would turn on the TV and we'd sit beside each other on her bed and sing along to the theme song, which I knew very well because it was my daughter Molly's favorite show, too. When it was over, we'd make up silly songs on my ukulele. Tina loved when I sang silly songs.

At the end of our visits, I'd give Tina stickers. That's how we knew it was time to say goodbye. It was always so hard to leave because her face dropped to such a degree I could feel the pressure change in the room. She'd watch for me while I made my way out of the unit and around to the big glass elevators at the center of the inpatient wing. I'd search the rows of windows for hers, and when we spotted each other she'd wave, face pressed against the glass. I'd blow kisses as the elevator descended, until she was out of sight.

·   ·   ·

I have a vivid memory of showing up one time when Tina was in distress. Her dad was trying to comfort her while her mom was trying to leave. She was hysterical, sobbing and screaming "Mama, mama!" and clawing at her mother at the door. Her parents tried to get her excited to see me but she was in the midst of heartbreak, and there is no soothing heartbreak until a space opens up for something else to enter and shift the experience. That can't be forced, so I just waited and breathed. I let her know that I was there, that I saw her, that I knew she was sad, and that it was okay. Her mom slipped out, tears in her eyes, and her dad moved to the back of the room so I could sit with Tina on the edge of her bed. She cried really hard for a few minutes.

I breathed out my fear of not being enough, of not knowing what to do, and I breathed in her beautiful brown eyes and the particular quality of the sorrow making her face scrunch. As I took in the exactness of the moment and I let go of the need for it to be any different, I noticed that I could see all of Tina simultaneously—the hurting part as well as the bright, resilient, joyful light behind the tears. I noticed that Tina was, and this moment was, despite appearances, innately and profoundly okay. I didn't need to change her, nor could I. Didn't pressure her to be or do anything different. I strummed my uke, poorly, the three or four chords I knew. I hummed and listened for the music.

Eventually, the space opened. Something softened. Silliness entered the room on a stream of ridiculous lyrics, peppered with a few "poops," knowing the sense of humor of the four-year-old beside me. She took my hand when she was ready, and we climbed together out of the sadness and into a song that loosely resembled a bad rendition of the Wiggles. Before long, Tina was jumping on the bed, laughing. This remains one of the clearest examples of magic in my memory, and one of my most treasured lessons. There is power in presence without judgment or demand, in the offering of loving friendship, and in a gentle invitation into playfulness when the time is right.

Making my way back to the dressing room, I had a mixed feeling in my belly that day. I felt good about the time I'd just spent with Tina, the quality of presence I had been able to bring to our play, but the look on her face as I'd dropped out of sight tugged at my heart. I wished I could do more, visit more often, stay longer, but there were so many children to see and only so much time. So many rooms to enter, all full of complicated experiences—the deep and natural joy of childhood mixed with the trauma of illness or injury. Beautiful, difficult, untidy experiences for which none of us can prepare.

And then there is the promise of death. Not in every room, but in enough of them, and maybe not today, but for many of these children it would come far sooner than we would wish. It hangs in the air of this place like a thickness and coats the floors with a sticky grip that makes it hard to move from room to room with a light step, but I keep trying to lift my feet, to pirouette and skip.

So as the elevator descended, I carried Tina with me in my heart, but I also tried to leave her behind. It's a strange and sad thing to share such an intimate experience with someone and then work to let it go, to be always here, now. And here, now. Here. Now. I wanted to leave this place clear, light, empty, so I could bring the same amount of presence home to my daughter. I couldn't wait to get home to see Molly, to hold her, but I was tired, and the last thing I wanted to do was play. Sometimes the emptiness feels pretty heavy.

I told my husband I was going to be late from work, that he'd have to give our daughter dinner, and I stopped at our local coffee shop to be by myself and stare at the wall. On the wall was an art exhibit—a collection of abstract paintings, speckled and splattered, colors dripped and thrown across clean white canvases. As I stood in front of the constellation of pieces hung on the barn board wall and stared quietly, wide-eyed, at each bright, lovely, chaotic burst, a flood of emotion rose in my chest and throat: delight, and gratitude, for the wild "is-ness" of each. For the perfect, lovely chaos. For the uncontrolled, pointless exuberance—each free to be as it is just for the sake of itself, not because it needed to mean something, or to be figured out. It looked like the artist had fun making them, and I wanted my life to be this way: beautiful, even if untidy. Good, even if I couldn't wrap my head around it.

Then it hit me. Maybe my life is this way; maybe that's why I was standing, my face a foot from a canvas, with an open-mouthed smile and tears rolling down my cheeks. I scanned the wall and located the small, white tag with the name of the collection typed neatly in black print: *These Beautiful Messes.* Yes. I handed over some money and took home two cards. One was an explosive fiery print, orange and red and yellow, with the words *There is no shadow you can't light up* curled across the front like a ribbon in the wind. The other was a swirly, aquamarine pearl that conjured the Mediterranean, with whitecap calligraphy front and center declaring *It is well with my soul.* I tucked them inside my coat and headed home, having gotten what I hadn't known I was going there for.

•   •   •

Tina's condition has deteriorated quickly, and she's been moved into reverse isolation on the bone marrow transplant unit. Her immune system is so compromised from the cancer treatment that a cold could kill her. She doesn't turn her head to watch me goof around with my gown anymore. I can't bring bubbles or stickers or my ukulele into her room now; only the bare minimum of essential supplies is allowed. Even if she felt like building a fort, there's no sofa.

A loud ventilation system set into the ceiling removes dangerous contaminants from the air, but also makes it hard to hear each other. Lip reading is impossible because of our masks, so the subtleties of communication are sucked out by the vacuum in the ceiling, along with the rest of the air. Only my eyes are left to express and respond, and they burn like spinning tires trying to move a load too heavy for their build.

Her mom and dad try to be upbeat, desperately grasping for any bit of joy they can give her. "Look Tina, Rose is here!" But Tina doesn't smile much anymore. She's sad, weak, and in pain. She's very close to the end. Most of the time she lies on her side, curled up with her eyes closed, and I crouch at the edge of her bed and talk to her quietly; but the noise from the vent drowns out my words, which is probably for the best because I don't know what to say anyway. Once in a while I sing her a silly *a capella* song that doesn't make her laugh anymore. She still wants me to come, so I do, but not as often as I should, and when I do come, I feel like I have nothing to offer.

•   •   •

It's Tina's birthday. She's finally five. And I just saw her for the last time. Before running back here to the dressing room to hide, I sang her happy birthday, and pretended that the song had the power to make it so. I left out the lilting post script "and many more." Looking at the untouched kindergarten worksheets stuck to the whiteboard across from her bed, I tried to hold back my tears, because crying in front of a patient is unprofessional.

I didn't know what to do, because at the heart of clowning, as I understand it, its essence is honesty and vulnerability. We embrace the full spectrum and depth of the human experience in order to invite others in. And we play the experience. In the therapeutic context, we nudge the intolerable, get inside it and find any bit of fun that can be squeezed out for nourishment. But this is too scary to feel in public, and too big to play. And Tina is no longer able to be my playmate.

I miss her already, and I'm sorry that I have nothing to give her as a goodbye present. Presence and friendship used to be enough, but it doesn't seem that way anymore. And I couldn't breathe in that room. And I don't feel like a clown. All this time, over all our hundreds of hours together, I've been able to hold Tina's sadness, but I don't know how to hold mine.

Sitting heavy in my chair, I squeeze my thumb to keep the drop of blood at the corner of my cuticle from spilling. The door opens, and Jamie—or A. Leboo more accurately, as his red nose and silliness are still in place—walks into the dressing room. He parks his toy cart, wipes the sweat off his forehead, and pulls a "slinky pop toob" out of a pocket under his tutu, stretching the musical accordion toy open to its full length so it makes a deep, warbly, elongated sound like a whale burp, and smiles at me.

"You're an idiot," I say, and smile back at him.

"Thanks," he says, and sits down across from me, lifting his red nose to rest on his forehead like a pair of sunglasses.

"I can't do this anymore," I say. "I think I have to quit."

There are a few seconds of silence, and then he says, "Don't quit. Take a medical leave." Apparently he is more aware of my visible signs of burnout—the ones I try so hard to hide—than I give him credit for. I haven't even considered a medical leave, but it makes sense.

I have no idea what kind of care I need, or if I will ever be able to serve again the way I used to—the way Rumi suggests in the weathered copy of my favorite poem taped inside my coffee cupboard, my personal manifesto of which I remind myself each morning as I reach for a mug: *Be a lamp, or a lifeboat, or a ladder. Help someone's soul heal. Walk out of your house like a shepherd.*

The red nose hanging around my neck, resting just above my ribs and matching the muscle inside that keeps me alive, has served for almost a decade as my shepherd's clothes. It's given me the honor of, and the opportunity to, show up. *Really* show up. To be a mirror for people whose circumstances are such that they desperately need to have their wholeness reflected back to them. Letting go of this small but significant piece of round, red rubber breaks my heart, but I don't feel whole right now, and I'm not a good mirror anymore. From where I sit, I can't tell if I ever will be again.

But maybe if I show up for myself and wait, hand outstretched, and just keep breathing, I'll get the chance to see. If I listen for what's needed, wait for a space to open and lean into it, maybe I'll be able to feel my way back toward wholeness. Maybe I can remember to recognize the perfection inherent in even the messy moments, like these. The painful ones that in no way feel okay, the ones I don't understand, that I wasn't prepared for. Maybe I need to let myself be shepherded for a while.

I let out the breath I hadn't realized I was holding. "Okay," I say, and turn to look at the pigeons.

FOR AIR
JENNIFER HU

On Monday, the naked woman was struggling for air.
Her blue gown hung at her ankles.
We had a name for her: Cachexia.
Cachexia. Hypoxia. Coma.
Words ending in "a" had always been beautiful to me.

The boy in bed #19 panted.
His skin glowed.
The room was of dying bowel & salt & rimmed with reluctant eyes.
I opened & closed the door so many times—each morning, each afternoon.
Change arrived, from nothing to everything.

I drove through the back roads to the woods.
I stood beneath impossible February weather.
My feet blistered, but I could feel and feel safe.
A stranger came, I pet his dog, & we spoke of the mountains.

After, I watched the sun set over the pond.
I rubbed the mud from my boots & drove home.
White magnolia, lone nostalgia, small panacea.

SECTION FOUR
DISCUSSION AND PROMPTS

A TRIBUTE (AND HOMAGE TO E E CUMMINGS)

Read e e cummings's poem "[i carry your heart with me (i carry it in]." How does the form and structure of Lenkov's poem relate both to her subject and cummings's original?

What is the "occult frailty / The great humbler" in this poem? Discuss the hidden defects or wounds of the heart this poem suggests to you.

✎ *Write about what you carry.*

NAMELESS

"*Be a doctor,* one of my mentors used to say. *You have the power of influence, the power of narrative.*" What do you think the mentor meant by this? Point out imagery of violence, silence, tenderness. Discuss power structures in Fleishman's story.

Discuss the multiple layers of grief present for the narrator in "Nameless." How do you suppose the narrator's experience would have been different had the connection between patient and family been different, or the connection between practitioner and family? The narrator says, "I could control the moment and tenor of her daughter's death, could enable an intimate touch between mother and child. But I could not help her." Discuss whether the narrator did or did not help the mother.

✎ *Write to someone nameless.*

PASSING THROUGH

Look at specific language the narrator uses to characterize Nathaniel Deacon. What details does the narrator offer about him? Compare this characterization of Deacon with that of the patient in Kantola's story, "Helping You." How do these characterizations illuminate the narrators' grief?

Despite Nathaniel Deacon's "frequent flier" status at the hospital, he is not understood by the people there, according to the speaker, a caseworker: "They know him as a cluster of signs and symptoms and an array of bad behaviors." Which systems in healthcare perpetuate this kind of limited vision of patients?

"This, I thought, is how the poor die now. They die from protocols, efficiencies, best practices, and criteria inherent in the machinery and money of medicine." How do you think factors such as race, socioeconomic status, adverse childhood experiences, and gender impact how patients die?

Throughout his story Bocchicchio writes of Nathaniel Deacon's falls. Talk about the allusion of falling.

✎ *Write about falling.*

YOU LEAVE THE ROOM

French's poem uses imagery of sight, sound, and touch to recount the moment immediately after losing a patient. Find and discuss the sensations described. Explore French's attention to sound in this poem. How does his use of techniques such as alliteration, assonance, consonance, and internal rhyme deepen your experience of the poem's emotional content?

Reread the poem and substitute the second person perspective with first person. How does this change the poem? Why do you suppose French chose to write in second person?

✎ *Using only sensory details, write about an emotion without naming it.*

A BIT IN THE TEETH

"Even when a patient and I did share moments of powerful significance—as I had with Frank—the black parade of new cases drowned out the feeling." Discuss Al-Mondhiry's metaphor "a black parade of new cases" and its impact on his affective experience with patients. Why does he go back and read through his notes? The last statement of the essay is a question: "Would he still love me anyway?" Discuss the significance of this question.

Al-Mondhiry allows readers access to the narrator's thoughts during dialogue with the patient. What internal monologue can you imagine for the patient? His family members?

✎ *Write about what is unsaid.*

A BEAUTIFUL MESS

"Full of passion, purpose, and optimism, I had no room in myself for death or any other endings back then, and I hadn't yet learned that the tender place behind my sternum might require more than bone for protection." Does Mannion's narrator make room in herself for death? If so, how? How have you made room in yourself for death? Describe what the tender place behind the sternum requires in order to make room for death.

Mannion writes about the role of a therapeutic clown as being a "mirror for people whose circumstances are such that they desperately need to have their wholeness reflected back to them." But, she says, "...I don't feel whole right now, and I'm not a good mirror anymore." What happens when what you feel inside is in conflict with what you're expected to give or provide professionally?

✑ *Write about shepherding or being shepherded.*

FOR AIR

In Hu's poem, the speaker's need for air mirrors that of her patients. How does she find it? Trace the mirroring of patient and healthcare professional that occurs in stories and poems throughout this book. How does the capacity for "mirroring" deepen or complicate the caregiving experience for you? For patients? Describe this in the context of power structures currently in place in healthcare. Describe this in the context of grief.

Pay attention to setting in Hu's poem. Discuss the line: "I could feel and feel safe."

✑ *Write about feeling safe.*

CONTRIBUTOR BIOGRAPHIES

JAFAR AL-MONDHIRY, MD, MA, is currently a hematology/oncology fellow at UCLA David Geffen School of Medicine in Los Angeles, CA. He completed his internal medicine residency and medical school at NYU, and earned his Master of Arts in Philosophy from Penn State University. His academic efforts reflect a broad interest in the medical humanities, with works in creative nonfiction, medical history, and medical ethics, and an overarching commitment to medical education. Dr. Al-Mondhiry's current work focuses on advancing palliative care education within oncology training.

SHANNON ARNTFIELD, MSC, MD, FRCSC, is an ob/gyn interested in the power of narrative in medicine. She lives in London, Ontario. This is her first published poem.

DANIEL BECKER MD, MPH, MFA, is Professor Emeritus at the University of Virginia School of Medicine, where he practiced and taught internal medicine until he retired in 2018. He now practices and teaches internal medicine as a volunteer. Dr. Becker says what had been part time is now close to full time on the phone or with Zoom, thanks to COVID-19.

CHRISTOPHER BLAKE, BA, MSC, MD, CCFP (PC), is a palliative care physician and writer from Ontario, Canada. His first literary loves are science fiction and fantasy, but he also enjoys more unconventional general fiction. He writes poetry, general and speculative fiction, and creative nonfiction. His academic interests include education, narrative medicine, wellness, and public health palliative care. Dr. Blake loves the opportunities the medical humanities offer to fuse his appreciation of medicine and the arts.

JOSEPH BOCCHICCHIO, BA, PHES, spent twenty-five years working in mental health and crisis intervention. His creative writing has been published in several journals including *Ovunque Siamo* and *Upstreet*, and the Edith Chase Symposium chapbooks, *River of Words* (2017) and *Resurrection River Poems* (2019). Two of his translations of work by the Haitian poet Charlot Lucien are included in a new trilingual anthology of contemporary Haitian poetry called, *This Land, My Beloved/ Ce Pays, mon amour.* Mr. Bocchicchio facilitated poetry workshops with marginalized women in collaboration with Nikki Robinson of the Wick Poetry Center at Kent State through the Bridges out of Poverty Program.

LILA FLAVIN, MD, is a psychiatry resident at NYU Langone. During medical school, she took a year off to learn to write and found that it was a way to synthesize the experiences in the hospital and feel whole again. She grew up in Boston and attended medical school there before moving to New York City for residency. Dr. Flavin lives in Brooklyn with her partner and Chihuahua and is currently at work on her first novel. Her essays and short stories have appeared in the *Journal of General Internal Medicine*, *Evocations*, and *Torrid Literature Journal*.

RACHEL FLEISHMAN, MD, is an academic neonatologist who writes creative nonfiction. Through her writing, she hopes to highlight aspects of humanism in the care of the patients and families she serves. Her essays have appeared in publications such as *The Philadelphia Inquirer*, *JAMA*, and *Literary Mama*.

SERENA J. FOX, MD, is an intensive care physician. She works at the Mount Sinai Beth Israel Medical Center in New York City. She has also served as a consultant in bedside medical ethics and a human rights advocate with Physicians for Human Rights. She believes deeply that poetry and the humanities have essential roles in the teaching of medicine and care giving. Her book of poems, *Night Shift* (Turning Point, 2009), is the basis for a series of poetry and medicine seminars that she facilitated first for the NYU School of Medicine Master Scholars Program and then the University of Iowa School of Medicine's Examined Life Conference: Writing and the Art of Medicine. She is the poetry editor for *The Examined Life Journal*.

WILLIAM A. FRENCH, MA, RRT, is a retired respiratory therapist and professor emeritus. He has more than thirty years of bedside experience and thirty-seven years of classroom experience, having moonlighted for many years. He holds degrees from Ohio State and The University of Chicago and has published multiple works, including *Breath of Life: Poems and Stories from the Front Lines of Health Care*.

JENNIFER HU, MD, is a psychiatry resident at Cambridge Health Alliance in Massachusetts. She graduated from University of Rochester School of Medicine, where she co-founded its literary and arts journal, *murmur*, with a fellow medical student. Her work has been published in the *Journal of Medical Humanities*, *Main Street Rag*, and *Thrush Poetry Journal*. Dr. Hu is the recipient of the Alpha Omega Alpha Student Poetry Award as well as the Bea Gonzalez Prize for Poetry awarded by *Stone Canoe: A Journal of Arts, Literature and Social Commentary*.

SIMONE KANTOLA, MD, practiced plastic and reconstructive surgery prior to transitioning to a career in medical education. She currently writes medical education content by day and stories for children by early morning. Now with a pen instead of a scalpel, she hopes to wield the power of words to inspire reflection and promote healing.

PAM LENKOV, MD, is a clinician at Women's College Hospital and at Sunnybrook Health Sciences Centre in Toronto. She is also an educator and Assistant Professor in the Department of Family and Community Medicine at University of Toronto.

MARY C. LINDBERG, MDIV, is an ordained Lutheran pastor who currently serves as chaplain at Columbia Lutheran Home in Seattle, WA. She earned her Master of Divinity degree from Pacific Lutheran Theological Seminary and did her chaplain residency training at Lutheran General Hospital in Chicago. In addition to her chaplaincy work with older adults, Reverend Lindberg has worked with patients at Seattle Cancer Care Alliance. She has a Writing Certificate from Northwestern University and an Editing Certificate from University of Washington. Her ministry has included writing for children and adults. Reverend Lindberg and her husband have two grown daughters.

TEEGAN MANNION is an award-winning poet, memoirist, and writing workshop leader certified in the Amherst Writers & Artists Method. Her work has appeared in *Another Dysfunctional Cancer Poem Anthology*. She is also a mother, a flower farmer, and a therapeutic clown. After training at the Tooba Physical Theatre Centre in Vancouver where she discovered her (ironic) love for the art of clowning (having disliked clowns as a child), she worked for years at SickKids Hospital in Toronto as a therapeutic clown in the Creative Arts Therapy Program. Clowning continues to provide her with a cherished paradigm for life. She is currently raising her babies and facilitating writing groups.

VENETA MASSON, MA, RN, has practiced nursing for thirty-five years, twenty of them in primary health care. She was a founder, director and, for most of two decades, family nurse practitioner in a small, mom-and-pop clinic providing office and home care to an inner-city neighborhood in Washington, DC. Out of that rich and intense experience, she began to keep a journal and, eventually, to write poems and essays. Her most recent collection of poetry is *Clinician's Guide to the Soul*. More of her work can be found at www.sagefemmepress.com.

PAMELA A. MITCHELL, MFA, RN, lives in Bend, Oregon. She is a nurse who teaches and consults in geriatric care. Her poems appear in *The Healing Muse, Pulse: Voices from the Heart of Medicine* and others as well as the anthologies *Intensive Care: More Poetry and Prose by Nurses* and *Water Writes.* She taught writing at SUNY Adirondack Community College, as well as journaling and poetry with psychiatric patients at Saratoga Hospital. She received a National Organization for Women award for her work with AIDS patients. Ms. Mitchell holds an RN from Upstate Medical Center in Syracuse, an MFA from Goddard College, and attended seminary at Church Divinity School of the Pacific in Berkeley, CA.

RICHARD MORAND, MD, FACS, has practiced general surgery for thirty-five years, including eight as a trauma surgeon at Scripps-Mercy Hospital Level 1 Trauma Center in San Diego, CA. He is a veteran of the US Navy and served with 2nd Marine Division during the first Iraq War. Dr. Morand is Associate Professor of Surgery at Dartmouth Medical School and most recently served as Chief of Thoracic Surgery at Togus Veterans Administration Hospital, Augusta, ME. He is a graduate of University of Rochester School of Medicine and completed a surgical internship and residency at Naval Medical Center San Diego, CA. Dr. Morand lives with his wife and son in Manchester, ME.

KACPER NIBURSKI, MA, MDCM (IN PROGRESS), is a third-year medical student at McGill University, an occasional writer, and sincere reader. You can follow his work at kacperniburski.com.

PAIVI E. PITTMAN earned a Bachelor of Arts in English with a Creative Writing focus from Boise State University. She previously worked as a pharmacy technician in a local hospital in Boise. While attending writing classes, she discovered a voice for the trauma she experienced not only in the hospital setting, but in childhood as well. Her writing often explores the complexities of trauma. Ms. Pittman lives in Boise with her nineteen-year-old cat.

ANEESH RAJMAIRA, MD, grew up in Marion, IN, with his twin sister and two loving parents. Having physicians as parents, he saw at an early age the rewards and sacrifices that come with a life in medicine. After high school, he attended Emory University and eventually found his own calling in medicine. He graduated from Indiana University School of Medicine and is pursuing his training in Emergency

Medicine at Stony Brook University. Affectionately called Neeshu by his family and close friends, Dr. Rajmaira considers himself to be a fun loving and free spirit. He enjoys the outdoors, playing guitar and piano, and a good laugh with loved ones. Dislikes include early bedtimes and strict planning.

SHERI REDA, MA, MAR, MLIS, is a writer, educator, presenter, and certified master life-cycle celebrant. She is also a certified spiritual director and mediator. She is a steering committee member of the Narrative Medicine Committee at Advocate Healthcare Park Ridge, IL, a board member at the C.G. Jung Center in Evanston, IL, and a member of the Chicago Conservation Corps. Ms. Reda presents talks, workshops, and seminars throughout the United States and in England. Her essays, poems, and stories are available through Moria Press, *Thread*, *Literate Ape*, and other publications in the United States and the UK.

LARA RONAN, MD, is an Associate Professor of Neurology and Medicine at Geisel School of Medicine, Dartmouth College and Vice-Chair for Education in the Department of Neurology at Dartmouth-Hitchcock in Lebanon, NH. She directs the DH Neurology Residency Program and has research interests in the intersection between the arts and humanities and medicine.

HUI-WEN ALINA SATO, RN, MSN, MPH, CCRN, currently practices as a pediatric ICU nurse in Los Angeles. She blogs regularly for the *American Journal of Nursing (AJN)* in their blog, *Off the Charts*. Her writing has also been published in *The Oxford Handbook of Meaningful Work*, *Intima*, and the Reflections column for *AJN*. In September 2017, she delivered a TEDxTalk titled "How Grief Can Enable Nurses to Endure," and she has been featured as a keynote speaker at numerous national nursing conferences. She is currently pursuing her Certificate of Professional Achievement in Narrative Medicine through Columbia University. She lives in Los Angeles with her husband, two children and two ornery tortoises. You can find more of her writing at http://heartofnursing.blog.

THOM SCHWARZ, RN, CHPN, has been an RN since 1978, working in hospice and palliative care for the past fourteen years. He says it's nice to find one's calling at the end of a career.

ELENA SCHWOLSKY, RN, MPH, is a nurse, activist and writer who spent a decade as a pediatric AIDS nurse at the height of the epidemic. Her essays have appeared in the *American Journal of Nursing* and *The Veteran Journal,* and her work has been included in the anthologies *Storied Dishes: What Our Family Recipes Tell Us About Who We Are and Where We've Been* and *Reflections on Nursing: 80 Inspiring Stories on the Art and Science of Nursing.* Her debut memoir, *Waking in Havana: A Memoir of AIDS and Healing in Cuba,* was published in November 2019 by She Writes Press.

KATHERINE DIBELLA SELUJA MSN, CPNP, is a poet and a nurse practitioner. She is the author of *Gather the Night* (UNM Press, 2018), a poetry collection that focuses on the impact of mental illness. Katherine is co-author, with Tina Carlson and Stella Reed, of the collaborative poetry collection, *We Are Meant to Carry Water* (3: A Taos Press, 2019). Katherine's poems have appeared in the *American Journal of Nursing, bosque, The Fourth River, Intima, Santa Fe Literary Review* and *Sin Fronteras,* among others. Katherine works in ambulatory pediatrics at Española Hospital and as adjunct clinical faculty for the University of New Mexico College of Nursing.

HOWARD F. STEIN, PHD, is an applied, psychoanalytic, medical, and organizational anthropologist, psychohistorian, organizational consultant, and poet. He is Professor Emeritus in the Department of Family and Preventive Medicine, University of Oklahoma Health Sciences Center, Oklahoma City, OK, where he taught for nearly thirty-five years. Dr. Stein has authored or edited thirty-two books, of which ten are books or chapbooks of poetry. He has most recently published a book of poems titled *Centre and Circumference* (MindMend Publishing, 2018). He is Poet Laureate of the High Plains Society for Applied Anthropology.

DANIEL J. WATERS, DO, MA, is a native of southern New Jersey and serves as Adjunct Professor of Medical Humanities at Des Moines University College of Osteopathic Medicine. He graduated from St. Joseph's College in Philadelphia and the University of Medicine and Dentistry of New Jersey and published his first story in 1981. His work has appeared in *JAMA, The New Physician, The Examined Life Journal, Intima,* and *Typishly Literary Magazine.* He practiced open-heart surgery for thirty years and has authored two collections of surgical advice as well as four novels. He holds a Graduate Certificate in Narrative Healthcare and a Master of Arts in Writing from Lenoir-Rhyne University in Asheville, NC.

KELLEY WHITE, MD, is a pediatrician who has worked in inner city Philadelphia and rural New Hampshire. Her poems have appeared in *Exquisite Corpse, Rattle,* and *JAMA.* Her recent books are *Toxic Environment* (Boston Poet Press, 2008) and *Two Birds in Flame* (Beech River Books, 2010.) She received a 2008 Pennsylvania Council on the Arts grant.

RONDALYN VARNEY WHITNEY, PHD, OTR/L, FAOTA, is an associate professor and Director of Faculty Scholarship and Development in the Division of Human Performance at West Virginia University (WVU) School of Medicine. Her scholarship focuses on the use of writing as a health practice with emphasis on promoting maternal and child health. She is currently completing a certificate in Narrative Medicine at Columbia University, has authored seven books, is widely published in the profession of occupational therapy and her poetry has appeared in several journals including *Yankee.*

ANNA-LEILA WILLIAMS, PHD, MPH, PA-C, is Professor of Medical Sciences at the Frank H. Netter MD School of Medicine at Quinnipiac University where she leads curriculum content in public health, social determinants of health, and narrative medicine. Dr. Williams received her PhD and PA from Yale University and completed post-doctoral training in psycho-oncology/palliative medicine at Dartmouth College Geisel School of Medicine. Her book, *Integrating Health Humanities, Social Sciences, and Clinical Care: A Guide to Self-Discovery, Compassion, and Well-being* (2019), is published by Routledge, Taylor & Francis.

MARIA WOLFE lives and writes in northeast Ohio, where she also practiced as a surgical specialist. This is her first publication of nonfiction. She has written academic works under her real name. Her fiction has appeared in *The Examined Life Journal, Please See Me,* and *Coffin Bell.*

A GUIDE FOR USING
THE HEALER'S BURDEN IN GROUPS

This book has been divided into four thematic sections, each with discussion questions and writing prompts, for use in narrative medicine workshops, medical humanities programs, reflective practice groups, and professional development sessions. Below are a few recommendations for facilitating such workshops or sessions.

- Respect your participants' schedules by selecting pieces that fit your allotted time frame. A one-hour time slot would allow reading and discussing a longer selection and then writing and sharing, whereas a thirty-minute slot might require the contemplation of a shorter piece. Sessions based on this material might be structured in a variety of ways that work for your setting and circumstances.
- Create an emotionally safe space by welcoming and respecting all voices. Pay attention to the physical space, and as much as possible, set a comfortable tone. Minimizing distractions, beginning and ending on time, and maintaining focus during discussion all help participants experience emotional safety.
- Be clear about confidentiality at the onset of each session. How will it be practiced and what are its limits? Consider the importance of *confidentiality of the moment*. As Benaifer Bhadha writes, "Confidentiality of the moment is more than just agreeing not to report a story outside of the workshop space. It asks all participants to understand that, just because someone shares a story in a moment, it does not mean they will want to talk about it at a later moment...ask the teller's permission to ask about a story..." (Bhadha 135)
- The discussion questions are not intended to elicit correct responses; rather, they are designed to deepen the attention to the written work, expand self-awareness, and create connection among those present—attention, representation, and affiliation, in narrative medicine terms. It is best for facilitators and participants to approach the questions with curiosity and wonder.
- The writing prompts are intended to be used following discussion on each piece, with five minutes allotted to write to the prompt. They were purposely designed as "short, expansive invitations that aim to open the mind..." (Charon, A Framework for Teaching Close Reading 184)

- In responding to shared writing, encourage participants to be fully present to each teller. Consider and respond to aspects of story such as voice, tone, form, and perspective, outlining its effect on the listener; avoid asking the teller for more details, how it made them feel, or other probing questions that may be experienced as intrusive. It may be helpful to treat all shared work as fiction rather than assuming that participants are writing personal truth, and to refer to "the teller or narrator of the story" rather than "you" while responding. Avoid allowing respondents to turn the focus from the piece presented to themselves ("That reminds me of the time that I…"). Remember that the purpose of the sessions is reflection and communal engagement in attention to story, not group therapy, though often such engagement yields therapeutic benefit.
- The topic carries a heaviness with it that may elicit difficult emotional experiences or reactions to past trauma for participants. Plan how you will manage and respond to this. It may be helpful to have mental health resources available to offer in such situations.
- As a facilitator, approach your role as learner rather than expert. This will enhance emotional safety for participants and allow for greater creativity, self-awareness, and sense of community.

WORKS CITED

Bhadha, Benaifer. "Storytelling and Listening." Burack-Weiss, Ann,
    Lynn Sarah Lawrence and Lynne Bamat Mijangos. *Narrative
    in Social Work Practice: The Power and Possibility of Story.*
    New York: Columbia University Press, 2017. pp. 127–43.

Charon, Rita. "A Framework for Teaching Close Reading."
    Charon, Rita, et al. *The Principles and Practice of Narrative Medicine.*
    New York: Oxford University Press, 2017. pp. 180–207.

Charon, Rita. "Introduction." Charon, Rita, et al. *The Principles and
    Practice of Narrative Medicine.* New York: Oxford University Press, 2017. pp. 1–12.

Charon, Rita. "Narrative Medicine: a Model for Empathy,
    Reflection, Profession, and Trust." JAMA, vol. 286, 2001, pp. 1897–902.

Clark, Elizabeth J. "Understanding Professional Grief." n.d.
    Social workers help people help themselves.
    http://www.helpstartshere.org/?p=936

Frank, Arthur. *The Wounded Storyteller: Body, Illness, & Ethics,
    Second Edition.* Chicago: Univ Of Chicago, 2013.

Ryan, Kay. "Things Don't Have to Be So Hard."
    The Niagra River. New York: Grove Press, 2005.

Sanders, Scott Russell. "The Singular First Person." *Sewanee Review,*
    vol. 96, no. 4, 1988, pp. 658–672.

ACKNOWLEDGMENTS

We celebrate and thank our friends at the Examined Life Conference, held annually at the University of Iowa Roy J. and Lucille A. Carver College of Medicine, for creating a forum and an opening for work such as this. Special gratitude to Cathleen Dicharry and David Etler for helping this book find its home.

With profound appreciation for the contributors who responded to the invitation to courageously share their experiences, we say thank you. We are confident their stories and poems will empower other healers to tend their grief and that of their colleagues.

We gratefully acknowledge the periodicals in which the following pieces first appeared:

Geriatric Nursing: "Occupational Therapy"
Journal of General Internal Medicine: "Hair Clips for Esma"
The *Paris Review*: "The Angio"
Santa Fe Literary Review: "Formula for Wholeness"

Melissa would like to thank Mindy Davis Buell, Executive Director of Michael's Place, for affording her the time and opportunity to fully pursue the topic of professional grief, and for her support personally and professionally. She offers her deepest gratitude to her husband, Eric Fournier, and her children, Gabby and Will, for their abundant love, humor, and patience.

Gina recognizes the Sisters of the Third Order of Saint Francis for their guiding mission in healthcare, "to serve with the greatest care and love in a community that celebrates the gift of life." For their gracious help and mentorship, she thanks Kristi Kirschner, MD, Joseph Piccione, SThD, JD, and Elsa Vazquez-Melendez, MD, and she honors the creative and compassionate future doctors from the University of Illinois College of Medicine. Gina is deeply grateful to her friends and family, especially her four children, for their loving devotion and encouragement.

JMJ

ABOUT THE EDITORS

MELISSA FOURNIER, LMSW, works as the Program Director for Michael's Place, a nonprofit bereavement support center in Traverse City, MI, where she designs and facilitates grief support programs including Writing Through Loss, an ongoing writing workshop aimed at helping individuals shape their grief narrative. Melissa has worked in adult, pediatric, and perinatal hospice, mental health, and has been a featured speaker on end-of-life, bereavement, and ethics. She holds a Master of Social Work degree from the University of Michigan, a Bachelor of Arts in Psychology from Wayne State University, and a Certificate of Professional Achievement in Narrative Medicine from Columbia University. Her writing has appeared in *Dunes Review, The Sow's Ear Poetry Review, Pulse: Voices from the Heart of Medicine,* and *Medical Literary Messenger.* She is co-editor of *AFTER: Stories about Loss and What Comes Next* (Barnwood Books, 2019) and author of *Abruptio* (The Poetry Box, 2019).

GINA PRIBAZ, MFA, MA, is a clinical associate in the Departments of Internal Medicine and Pediatrics at the University of Illinois College of Medicine, where she teaches creative writing. She has developed health humanities, arts, and ethics programming at a nonprofit healthcare system in Peoria, IL. She holds an MFA in creative nonfiction from Northwestern University, a Master of Arts in Literature from the University of Iowa, and a Bachelor of Arts from the University of Notre Dame. Her essays have appeared in *Body and Soul: Narrative of Healing from Ars Medica, Tampa Review, Brain,Child Magazine,* and elsewhere. She volunteers with the National Organization for Arts in Health.

Please visit our website: **WWW.HEALERSBURDEN.COM**

ABOUT THE ARTIST

"There are those lonely moments when I feel exhausted, having fought for my patients with my last ounce of strength, having brought to bear all my years of experience and knowledge and discipline in an effort to save the patient's life."
— **JOE WILDER, MD (1920-2003)**

The artwork featured on the cover of this book is an adaptation of *Removing Gloves*, oil on canvas by Dr. Joe Wilder. We are deeply grateful to Madeline Stern Wilder for permission to use her late husband's work.

We could not imagine a more apt welcome into a book created for healthcare clinicians and founded on principals of narrative medicine than the artwork of a healer. Dr. Joe Wilder dedicated his life to alleviating human suffering through careful presence and attention to others. He was a graduate of Dartmouth College and earned his medical degree from Columbia University College of Physicians and Surgeons. He went on to serve as Chief of Surgery at Wright Patterson U.S. Air Force Base and The Hospital for Joint Diseases. Dr. Wilder was Professor of Surgery at Mount Sinai School of Medicine and Director of Emergency Services at Mount Sinai Hospital, New York. Dr Wilder authored two books on surgery and four books of artwork. Among his many accomplishments as a surgeon and artist, Dr. Wilder was awarded the Dartmouth College Presidential Inaugural Medal for Achievement in Art and Medicine. For more information about Dr. Joe Wilder, and to view complete renditions of his works, please visit https://joewilderarts.com and The National Library of Medicine at https://circulatingnow.nlm.nih.gov.

Made in the USA
Monee, IL
19 December 2020